A Celebration of
Banners

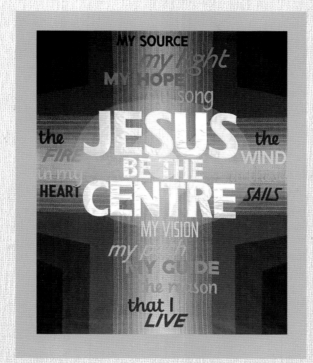

MY SOURCE
my light
MY HOPE
song
the
FIRE
JESUS
BE THE
CENTRE
the
WIND
HEART
SAILS
MY VISION
my
MY GUIDE
son
that I
LIVE

Edited and compiled by

Ruth Wood and Priscilla Nunnerley

ROCHART

Rochart, 69 Harlech Road, Abbots Langley, Hertfordshire, WD5 0BE UK

By Priscilla Nunnerley
An Army with Banners (published 1982)
Banners in His Name (published 1986)
Banner-Makers to the King (published 1989)

By Ruth Wood and Priscilla Nunnerley
Banners Around the World (published 1994)
Making and Using Banners (published 1998)

All these books are out of print and will not be reprinted.

If you want to base your banner on a design from the Good News Bible, as a matter of courtesy, you should first write to the Project Co-ordination Manager, Bible Society, Stonehill Green, Westlea, Swindon SN5 7DG for permission as they hold the copyright. In most cases permission will readily be given.

We are grateful to The Bible Society for their permission to print the Easter banner with its figures from the Good News Bible from Walton-on-the-Hill, Stafford.

If you wish to copy banners from Derby please ask Juliet Hemingway for permission (see Resources).

Design and origination by Roger Chouler, David Wiggins and Donna Pendrey
Published in 2008 for the authors by
Rochart, 69 Harlech Road, Abbots Langley, Herts, WD5 0BE
Tel: 01923 662806   E-mail: rchouler@aol.com

ISBN 978 0 9558582 0 8

British Library and cataloguing data
A catalogue record of this book is available from the British Library.

Printed on paper from sustainable forests by MWL Digital, Wales.

Acknowledgements

We would like to express our appreciation and gratitude to all who have a part in the book:

Those of you, from 55 places, who have given the best of your work, your thoughts and your photographs. **This is your book.**

The Pastors – for your support over the years, Stuart Reid, Ian Stackhouse and now our present pastor, Paul Lynch.

Rosas Mitchell (Priscilla's sister) from Stirling, whom we visited in June 2005 when she gave us fresh ideas and constructive criticism. We deeply appreciate her joyful, positive support`.

Grace Worthington – a good friend, for her interest, skill, patience and kindness in typing the manuscript during the last three years.

Rose Harvey – another good friend – for constant encouragement and willingness to send and receive e-mails and to receive digital pictures.

Gill Douglas from York, a good friend, for her wisdom, support and encouragement over many years in the writing of banner books.

Peter Flint – a good friend and strong support over many years.

Kate King at JMC Office Services, Prestwood for help with typing and printing digital pictures.

The Amersham Business Services for their friendly professional services in providing stationery materials and help with photocopying.

Tessa Spantan – a friend from Sutton, Surrey, who works with silk paints for help in contacting three people who work in this medium at Dagenham, Deanshanger and Derby.

Barbara Mann from Queensland whose friends in Darwin sent photos of a banner-making workshop.

Mark Russell who took over 50 banners from UK Christians as gifts to Albanian Churches, resulting in the making of banners there – a group at Durres have contributed a photo.

Valerie Main for banners from South Australia and for *David Patrick's* address, resulting in his contribution of photographs of paintings from Happy Valley near Adelaide.

Operation Mobilisation who put us in touch with *Simon Yeoman*, resulting in photos of the March for Jesus in Paris.

The South American Missionary Society who suggested we should write to *Canon John Cobb* in Santiago, Chile. He sent a picture of a banner made by his mother for St. Andrés Church.

Peter and Anne Dreyer from Limekilns, Fife, who spent a year travelling the world. While biking in Canada, they stopped for morning worship at St. Andrew's church in Sault St. Marie and photographed the patchwork banner displayed there. They also sent a picture of an anniversary banner from Wanaka, New Zealand.

Keith and Jenny Bates – friends in our church who visited Coventry Cathedral and returned with news of the beautiful Weddington banners displayed in an exhibition in a side chapel.

David Wood – who contributed the colours of the precious stones on the walls of the Holy City (p. 98).

We would finally like to thank *Roger Chouler* and his wife *Chris* for their kindness and hospitality. We are deeply appreciative of Roger's skills in preparing this book for print - and of making it fun to work with him.

Contents

Different Topics

Preface

An introductory light-hearted anecdote from Priscilla

Ruth and I have been friends over many years; she has been a great encouragement to me over years of banner-making and writing banner books. I once took her on a mystery trip to celebrate her birthday. We got a little lost on the London Underground and finally arrived at the Royal Albert Hall just in time to attend a Prom Praise Concert! Placing ourselves near the centre of the arena, I produced our banner from a bag, 'King of Kings and Lord of Lords'. This we waved at several appropriate moments. It was the most unusual of our travels with the banners.

We believe in a God who delights in his people enjoying art and who calls some to a specific work. This is seen with his instructions to Bezalel and his team for the design, measurements, colours and materials for the tabernacle (Exodus 31:1–11 and also chapters 25–30). We also read that David gave Solomon the plans of all that the Spirit had put in his mind for the courts and surrounding rooms of the later Temple, and the articles to be used in its service (1 Chronicles 28:11–13, 19 & 21).

Banner-makers, over many years, have experienced God's guidance in the process and his authority in the finished work. We have sought to prepare a place for his Spirit to come and his presence to be known.

We are so very grateful to all of you who have taken part making this book possible, trusting us with your photographs, comments and stories. It has been a real privilege to receive your letters, emails and phone calls, to look at your work, and so get to know you along the way.

Banner-making is for people of all ages and abilities. There are various practical tasks and many people, as part of their Christian experience and journey, may be given words of Scripture and images which can be used. Not all people who take part in groups are Christians; some come closer to Christ in times of creativity.

Our earlier 5 books are now all out of print (33,000 copies have been sold). In compiling this one we wanted to do something fresh. Waiting on the Lord in the autumn of 2002, we were encouraged to receive photographs of banners from two church groups and decided to send out letters to a number of addresses. In autumn 2003, we started work on material we had received, sending out further invitations as the project grew. We only met once a week, enjoying our varied lives and meeting friends in Amersham and family and friends elsewhere. Earlier we had been teachers, Ruth at secondary school and Priscilla at junior school.

Reading the contributions that accompanied the photos, we found a resonance in the way people found their inspiration for words and design. In it all, prayer, openness to the Word and waiting on the Lord are fundamental. Some have felt they were fulfilling a prophetic function. Generally prophecy simply means telling forth things about God and His Word. Sometimes banner-makers have felt they have, or have been given by others, specific ideas for the present situations – 'Rhema' or 'now' words. All need to be tested by the Spirit and the Scriptures. See a most helpful section in the chapter from York by Gill Douglas.

Many people work in groups, some appointing leaders and others working happily together in shared responsibility. We have let Harrogate and York tell their stories of groups in detail. Some people work alone – Burgh Heath speaks about this experience.

All banners are based on Scripture although not all use actual biblical words. 'Jesus be the Centre' is an example of this as are the Happy Valley paintings. Some people do not put Scripture references but others choose to include them. Our own comments have been added in boxes and on some full pages in italic script.

Four pages show the compassion of Christ for those in need. Deanshanger contributes a banner of a striking Christ figure who brings 'good news to the poor' and shows people leaving the darkness of despair for new life, healing and joy. Croxley Green and Stirling have movingly portrayed the parable of Matthew 25 with its challenge, that whatever we do for those who are suffering, we do it unto Christ himself.

Ruth writes:

> As a non banner-maker (I once cut out a rainbow coloured letter for a March for Jesus!) I have enjoyed seeing many of them and some have been of great significance to me.
>
> I remember, one Easter, seeing beneath the pulpit in our church, a very plain brown banner which had a cross outlined in gold cord. The words in the centre of the cross were simply "It is finished" and they shot through me, bringing conviction, deep gratitude, hope and joy.
>
> Another time, on holiday, I went with Priscilla and our friend, Angela, to a church gathered in a hall. On a wall to our right was a banner of a hillside with sheep and a shepherd. I saw it - but the service was soon to begin so I turned away. During the singing of a hymn - maybe the first one – I heard the Lord say my name and 'I am the Good Shepherd' three times. I was completely lost to my surroundings and now, years later, constantly hold on to those clear words, whatever my situation.

'Jesus be the Centre' – is the impetus behind this book. We see the making of Banners as a small part of fulfilling the Great Commission (Matthew 28:18–20).

Let us be open to the wonder of the vision and the greatness of the world beyond, which we lightly touch in making banners – the mystery of His being and His ways and the hints of surpassing glory yet to be revealed. There are increasing signs of Christ's predictions being fulfilled (Matthew 24, especially 4–8). May we be ready for his return.

Ruth Wood and Priscilla Nunnerley
The King's Church, Amersham, Buckinghamshire
February 2008

This day of waiting His return
Seems as a thousand years
It will be transmuted into Eternity
In His company, seeming too short a day

Ruth Wood

A Banner for Ghana

In 2002 a letter arrived from Kumasi, Ghana, asking for two large banners for the King's Church. The leaders, Edward and Mary Odame were so enthusiastic they insisted they would wait as long as necessary to receive the gifts. The request brought together a group not all of whom had worked on our banner team before and so resulted in a fresh approach.

The basis for the design of one of the banners was 'I have loved you with an everlasting love' (Jeremiah 31:3) given by Mary Odame. Pondering these words and praying for God to lead us the vision came of a constant river flowing from the Cross – representing God's love shown to us on the Cross, pouring out through the life of Jesus and His church.

In an interesting mix of hands-on creativity and technology, the design was sketched out and then redrawn on a computer. It was then enlarged, printed out and regrouped as with pieces of a jigsaw puzzle. This method allowed us to work in sections, each member of the group being responsible for a few of the twelve pieces of the image. The pieces were numbered so that they could be joined together easily.

We had two merry sessions surrounded by aqua-blue, blue, green and silver fabrics for the flowing waters, and woven brown material chosen for the Cross. The fabrics were cut using the printed segments as guides with extra allowances for hems. Some of the fabrics for the river were used flat, others were brunched and folded with the shape, adding a sculptured character to the water.

Using the numbered pieces we joined the jigsaw back together. The shapes were assembled on a circle of thin cotton and stitched on. The main background cotton fabric needed to be of a good weight to hang well with all the elements attached. For this we chose calico and made it up separately with some decorative fabric borders and with sleeves top and bottom to hold the poles. The design was stitched onto the centre of the background. Finally the letters were enlarged on a photo-copier and cut out in a dull gold bonded fabric and glued on with Uhu quick-sticking glue.

Completion! The banner measured 2m 18 cm x 1m 21 cm (7 ft 3 in. x 4 ft). It was hung in our chapel for a month. Then the banners (without poles) were folded and placed in simple cloth bags and taken as hand luggage to Ghana.

The church in Kumasi were delighted to receive the banners to further inspire their worship. The banner team enjoyed fellowship and great fun and an opportunity to share ideas and techniques. Supremely all shared in the everlasting love of God.

Luana Fowler, Susanna Stackhouse and friends
The King's Church

The Names of Jesus

The inspiration for this design came from a Christmas card where each name was in a different style. This is a simpler version. We chose the names for this banner, first made for Christmas but used for many occasions.

The background fabric is an attractive strong curtain material. It was machined with a sleeve top and bottom. The name of Jesus was enlarged onto tracing paper and then pins and tailor's chalk were used to transfer the lines on to the background fabric. The gold cord was couched on with a light double thread.

The other names were cut out in felt and glued on with a quick-sticking glue. Finally we notched a dowel rod at both ends for the cord and with delight, hung the banner in place. The banner measured 1.4m x 1.9m (4 ft 7 in. x 6 ft 3 in).

Marjorie Camble, Asuntha Pilendiram and
Priscilla Nunnerley, The Kings Church,
Amersham

Ayr, Ayrshire

Communion Banner – Invitation to a Feast

Inspiration for this banner came from the familiar scripture repeated every Sunday as we 'gather round the Lord's table' 'Do this in remembrance of me' (1 Corinthians 11:23–26).

As a group we felt that a visual reminder would keep us from taking it all for granted and would focus our thoughts on the awesome nature of our God, and how He has bought peace for us at such a cost. As an older song puts it:

See the feast of love divine
Broken bread and poured out wine

Some scriptures refer to the cross as 'the tree'. We pictured this as a rough trunk, not smoothly planed wood as 'The Carpenter' would have made it. Please note the scarlet thread – the blood of Jesus.

Some items on this banner are three dimensional – the grapes and the ears of wheat; the trunk is made with hand twisted cord and macramé.

A Cord of Three Strands is Not Quickly Broken (Ecclesiastes 4:12)

This banner was made to welcome Mark, one of our missionaries in Peru, who was bringing home his new wife, Violeta. The three flags hanging from the top represent God (King – Royal Purple), Mark (Scotland – Blue), and Violeta (Peru – Red). The circle is a symbol of God's love and protection. The three strands are combined to make a strong cord (any resemblance to a thistle is purely accidental!)

This banner travelled back to Peru with Mark and Violeta. We hope they understand it there!

Faith Robertson and friends, Ayr Baptist Church

Barnehurst, Kent

'Stations of the Cross' Project

Over the course of many visits to the Friars at Aylesford in Kent since 1993 I have become particularly drawn to the ceramic Stations of the Cross in St. Simon's Chapel.

Whilst there in July 1999 the thought came to me of making small banners of the Stations of the Cross. At first I said 'No, no! I can't do it. It's too difficult!' Then I thought about the people at the Bexley Centre for the Unemployed. Together we had made two banners and one altar frontal. Perhaps I could do it with them as a project to celebrate the Millennium? The more I thought about it, the more it seemed appropriate to ask for their assistance. Unemployed people and those suffering from mental health problems, know about rejection, some know about persecution and a few know about crucifixion in their own lives – all the things Jesus knew as he made his way to the Cross.

The Co-ordinator of the Centre agreed to the project and so we started, a group of six women and a man who helped us with the drawings. We studied how others had portrayed the stations and wanted to put our own stamp on the work so we tried to view some scenes from behind as in XII.

Once we started I found the easiest way of working was to prepare the figures at home and for the group to stitch these on to the banners. We had three colours for the background – blue, yellow and beige. Sometimes we added layers of net in other colours to give a different effect. The cross was made from an old curtain, the figures were made from scraps of material and the garment of Jesus was linen.

Some of the group were not Christians but really enjoyed working on the project. I felt deeply privileged to be part of it all and grateful for friends who prayed for us. By two weeks before Easter we had made eleven of the fifteen Stations and we presented them to the Rev. David Springthorpe, the Vicar of St. Martins, Barnehurst, the church where I worship. He was most appreciative. During the next two years I finished the other four banners at home. All are displayed in church for two weeks before Easter every year. I still get comments from members of the congregation of how much they like them.

Gill Sathyamoorthy, St Martins Church

Doreen, Agnes and Gill

The Stations of the Cross

Jesus is nailed
to the cross

Jesus speaks to his
mother from the cross

Jesus
dies on
the cross

Jesus is taken down
from the cross

Jesus is laid in
the tomb

Thank-you God

The Junior Church asked for help to plan and make a banner. As the age range was from three to fifteen years, it was decided it would be best to work in four groups. Each group was given one of the four seasons to illustrate and they created their own designs. The completed pictures were assembled to form the banner.

Children's ideas are often full of joy and vitality and far freer and more original than those of adults. Clear letters cut by an older person can complete a banner. Fairly strong non-stretch backgrounds are essential for banners when pictures are fixed onto them.

Harvest Banner

This banner is always displayed at the Harvest Festival. Most of the fruit and vegetables are padded giving the banner a three-dimensional effect. The hessian backing adds a rustic touch.

Kathleen Wilkinson and friends
Staincross Methodist Church

Banners in the Bible

These are selected from the references to banners in the Old Testament.

The Lord is my Banner (Exodus 17:15)

We will lift up our banners in the name of our God (Psalm 20:5)

His banner over me is love (Song of Songs 2:4)

The Root of Jesse will stand as a banner for the peoples; the nations will rally to him and his place of rest will be glorious (Isaiah 11:10)

All you people of the world, you who live on the earth, when a banner is raised on the mountains you will see it (Isaiah 18:3)

See, I will beckon to the Gentiles, I will lift up my Banner to the peoples. Those who hope in me will not be disappointed (Isaiah 49:22,23)

Prepare the way for the people
Build up, build up the highway!
Remove the stones

Raise a banner for the nations (Isaiah 62:10)

Lift up a banner in the land (Jeremiah 51:27)

Belfast, Northern Ireland

This banner was made for our minister's wife when she was the Belfast District President of the Methodist Women's Association in 1995/6. Her theme for the two years was 'Jesus, the Healer of hurts', particularly relevant to a city traumatised by 'the troubles' in Northern Ireland with so much lingering pain.

Madge Tarrant and friends,
Cregagh Methodist Church, Belfast

The inspiration for the banner came to them from the front cover of a book by Rev. Russ Parker of the Acorn Healing Foundation. We are grateful to him, together with the artist, Leigh Hurlock, and the publishers Darton, Longman and Todd for permission to print this banner.

Steps to Making a Banner

Pray together asking God to guide you

Ask these Questions
- *What is the intended size and shape?*
- *Will it be a swift/simple banner or a lengthy project?*

Early Planning Stages
1. *Inspiration – Page 22 – will give you various ideas*
2. *Decide on the words and/or design*
3. *Choose the lettering, deciding on a style that will give a suitable mood*
4. *Enlarge the design using a grid to square up or use a photocopier*
5. *Decide on the most suitable technique, appliqué, spray painting, dyeing, etc.*
6. *Choose the background colour and assign someone to buy the materials*
7. *Arrange times to meet and completion date*

During the Making
1. *Involve all the group. If you are more than six you may need to work in two groups so that everyone plays a part*
2. *Hold the half-completed banner at a distance to check*
3. *Line the banner if the material is thin*
4. *Machine sleeves at the top (and bottom too if desired)*
5. *Enjoy the friendship and fun. The relationships will last when the banners are tattered remnants*

Final Stage
Notch the ends of a dowel rod or cane so that the cord does not slip. Hang your banner in place. Fringes, tassles and more elaborate rods can be used if desired.

Jesus Christ is the same yesterday and today and forever (Hebrews 13:8)

Millennium Night Party guests were invited to write, on fabric patches, with fabric marker pens, what Jesus meant to them. These patches form the border. The rainbow colours in the centre of the banner are a reminder of God's promise. The self-adhesive felt letters are in styles to represent past, present and future.

Christ Jesus has destroyed death and brought life – Hallelujah (2 Timothy 1:10)

This was made for Easter. Paper stencils of the letters were placed on stiff white fabric and then car spray paints were applied. Next, the Cross was placed over the stencil letters and the spraying was repeated. Then all the stencils were removed and sequins and gold glitter glue were used to highlight round the base of the Cross.

Avril Norton and friends
Biggin Hill Christian Fellowship

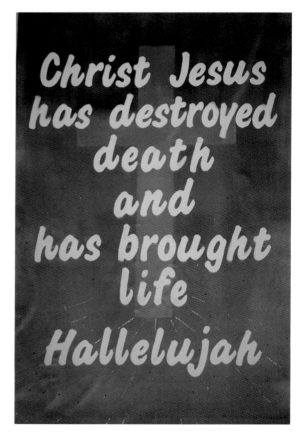

Jesus – salvation is found in no-one else (Acts 4:12)

This banner hangs high from the ceiling, against the wall. Car spray paint was applied over a paper stencil of the name 'Jesus', which had been pinned onto pre-washed calico. The smaller words were cut from two layers of black net and hand stitched on. The whole banner was backed with poly-wadding and more calico. Quilting around the word 'Jesus' was done by hand; the rest of the banner was machine quilted randomly. The whole was edged with loosely plaited braid.

**They devoted themselves to the apostles teaching and to the
fellowship, to the breaking of bread and to prayer** (Acts 2:42)

The picture is from a series of banners we made to go around our main church hall. Each is car spray painted on to a single layer of pre-washed calico, over templates cut from thin card. We used black Velcro to attach them – the hook side tacked to the wooden ceiling and the loopy side to the banners – so that they can be removed and replaced as necessary.

Avril Norton and friends, Biggin Hill Christian Fellowship

The Candle Banners

After a course for 'Church Banner Making and Prayer' I believed I received the idea 'Something for Christmas and over into Epiphany. Subject - light - candles as symbols.' I felt too there should be a challenge. Looking up every verse on light I chose John 3:19 and Ephesians 5:8 and planned two banners, one for each side of our communion table.

Strong backgound fabric was chosen. The single candle was padded and several shiny fabrics were used for the flame. For the small candles different materials were backed with adhesive Vilene, the edges zig-zagged and decoration added. Then they were attached. The flames needed to shine and so were cut from rolled mirror acetate. These wouldn't flattten so the ends curled freely once they were stitched in place! Alternatively holographic plastic could be backed and attached flat.

The other letters were cut out in paper, arranged so they fitted the desired shape, and cut out in white felt.

Gweneth Brooks – The Church of Ascension, Westdene
Jamet Killeen assisted with the word positioning

Praise and Proclamation banners

These banners were really a side product of beautiful evenings some 6–10 of us spent round the dining room table, sewing and chatting together. Sometimes there were tears but mostly there was laughter and enjoyment of each other's company. These were precious times. The banners meant much to us and the Lord was at the centre of all our planning. When we knew what He wanted we got started on His banners.

Diana Wood and friends, Brixham Baptist Church

Inspiration

Many banners will be straightforward. You do not need a long discussion on 'Praise the Lord' except perhaps on the practical details. Illustrations from His Word of proclamation, praise and promise which are constant and universal statements are appropriate at any time of year.

Other banners require special thought. In recent years, banner groups have become increasingly aware of their role in seeking the Lord for a word that is on His heart for the people. We have desired to capture His love, might and majesty and to receive a message from Him from the Word of God that will direct us ahead – a 'now' word that speaks to a specific group of people.

There are different ways of finding this word. You can choose the most appropriate:

- *Talking with your church leaders*
- *People bring words or designs they have been thinking about*
- *The group meditates on the Word during a time of quiet*
- *The group has a Bible study*
- *Others in the church contribute ideas*
- *Relevant objects or music are used to stimulate thought such as daffodils, a crown of thorns and Easter music*
- *A certain banner group usually sketches ideas on paper and then puts them all out on the table to consider. They often find a common theme coming through. If, on the odd occasion someone disagrees, they pray and rethink the design.*

When the group has a sense of rightness about certain words then those are the ones. The knowledge is an inner witness to the Holy Spirit speaking. You can sense Him, but He is like the wind and you can't predict or direct Him.

If there is any question or doubt, ask the Holy Spirit's confirmation, maybe by seeking the advice of the church leadership. One group, on meeting to make a Christmas banner, could not decide on anything and so felt the Lord wanted them to have more time for other things at that busy season.

From 'Banner-Makers to the King'

Burgh Heath and Cheam

Working as an individual

Although I'm in favour of banner groups and know they can be a great blessing to those involved, God has led me into an individual ministry designing and making some sixty banners over the last twenty years. Health and other commitments make it important for me to work at my own pace, picking up and putting down a project at a moment's notice. However I'm more than willing to share ideas and experience with others.

Continually dependent on the Holy Spirit for help and guidance, I pray at all stages of the procedure and then trust that the ideas that emerge, suddenly or gradually, are from God. Sometimes inspiration comes slowly and a process of trial and error may be involved; on other occasions (not many) I have a very clear plan. Friends pray for me and I frequently get constructive criticism from my husband. Ideas come from Bible verses, song words, sermons, the natural world, book illustrations, magazines, greeting cards, CD covers, other people's suggestions and sometimes other people's banners!

Christine Symes, St Paul's linked with St. Mary's

This small banner was made by way of encouragement for some friends, Brian, who has a full-time ministry among men in prisons, and his wife Jennie, who supports him as well as exercising her own gifts as a counsellor.

Knowing that this was a verse that meant much to them, I kept the banner simple for maximum impact. The strong rainbow colours (overlapping strips machined on to a dark blue background) convey God's faithfulness and the faint shape of a cross in white net shows through. The letters are cut from a satiny material giving a glowing effect. This and 'my peace I give you' are the smallest banners measuring 45 x 30 cm (1 ft 6 in.).

my peace

I give you

This is the day that the LORD has made

we will rejoice and be glad in it

THOSE WHO HOPE IN THE LORD

WILL RENEW

THEIR STRENGTH

ISAIAH 40:31

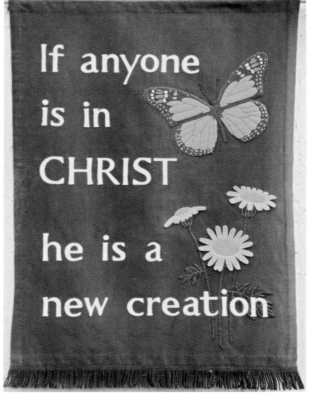

If anyone is in CHRIST he is a new creation

24

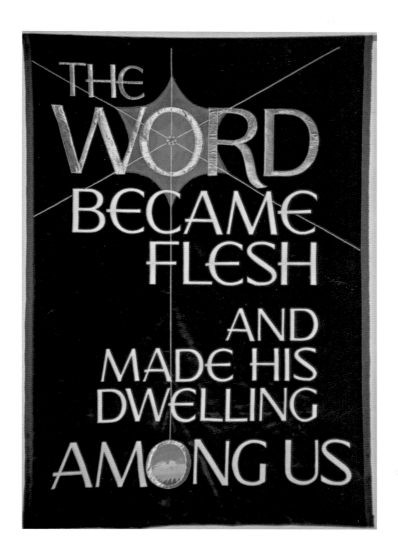

The Word Became Flesh

The material for this was a large piece of dark blue velvet that was given to me. I would probably not have gone out and chosen it as the thick pile makes it quite difficult to appliqué on to; however now that the work is done I just love its soft, rich texture.

This verse from John 1:14 epitomises the miracle and mystery of Christmas. The design appears simple but great care was required in planning the layout of the lettering so that the 'Os' would exactly line up vertically. The letters are gold and cream and the rays are gold cord. The star is cream net bondawebbed on to the blue velvet, with a gold leather and sequin centre. The dimensions of the banner about 180 cm by 130 cm (6 ft x 4 ft 4 in) and the large calligraphic lettering guarantee a strong impact right to the very back of a big building, while the detail of the image of the Christ-child can be appreciated at close range.

Praise God from Whom all Blessings flow

The theme was to be joyful praise, and the words of this ancient doxology which we now sing to a lively rock tune seemed just right. The swathe of music across the middle has the words and melody of lines 2 to 4 – the twirls at each end are a pair of black bootlaces! The colours were chosen very carefully to be varied and eye-catching but not riotous! I gave the large white satin letters a thin black edge (by bondawebbing them on to black felt) for maximum impact.

It took hours of detailed planning, concentrated work and faith to see this project through.

God of Creation we praise You

I wanted to design a banner expressing the beauty, colour and diversity of the natural world. God gave me the idea of the merging layers illustrating a variety of different habitats (coral reef, tropical rainforest, riverside and so on) and some of the creatures and plants contained in them. The stars and planets of outer space would surround on three sides the depiction of life on earth.

The pure white area has a superimposed satin cross with a crown, lamb and dove – white rays from this section extend to touch parts of the creation. Praise is conveyed by the upraised arms of the 'see-through' figures. Words from a modern worship song seemed appropriate.

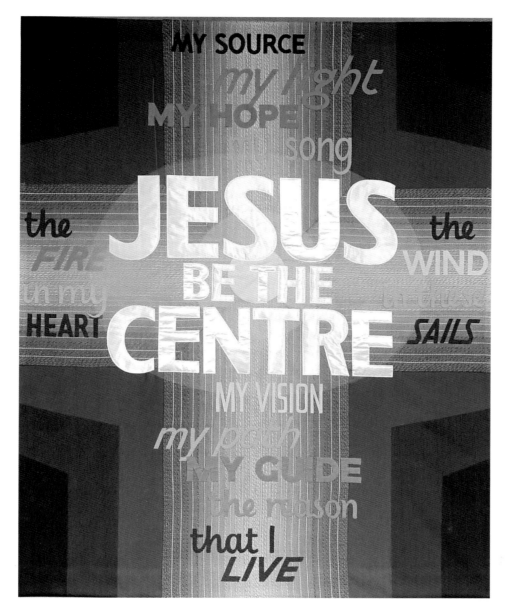

Jesus be the Centre

The words for this banner are taken directly from the lovely song by Michael Frye. For me they express my whole aim, in my banner-making and in my life.

The cross shape is carefully cut strips from curtain material with woven stripes in it discovered in the charity shop where I work. (I could see its potential for this sort of effect). The shades of brown in the four corner areas are achieved by overlapping pieces of brown net. The large letters are cut from satiny material; the light catches them and causes them to glow. The other words are cut from felt and other fabrics.

A variety of techniques were used to attach the letters including machine-stitching, hand-stitching and Bondaweb.

It was completed in time for the wedding of our Youth Ministers, Tom and Lesley. It has since been used for other weddings; with its neutral colours and strong message of commitment it seems particularly appropriate.   Song words by kind permission of Copy Care.

Banners with children

I have been involved for many years with creating banners to hang in Bushey Baptist Church. The majority of these were made with children from ages 5 to 11 during four or more days of a Holiday Club or at Sunday school.

The purpose of the banners is to raise up the name of Jesus. Through research, prayer and reflection, thoughts and images develop. The input of a talented friend, Margaret Farrell, has been invaluable. We discussed, made samples and then prepared well for the starting point. When the children arrived we encouraged them to add their ideas, drawings and choice of fabric. Together we stepped out in faith, creating as we went, as not all was revealed to us at the beginning.

Stitching is done enthusiastically by the children. The key is to match the colour of the thread closely to the item being stitched, often felt, and then the stitches do not need to be perfect. I encourage children to stitch in and out of lightweight fabric in one movement to avoid the thread being taken to the back and getting tangled. Many children can stitch at the same time. This work is mounted onto a sturdy fabric.

Self-adhesive felt was used for the lettering which was cut out by one of our house -groups. We cut narrow strips of the felt to edge some of the shapes.

Olympic banners

The Olympic rings were translated into horizontal bands of colour with the addition of white, black being encapsulated in the bold figures. Circles of felt were stitched on by the children within the bands.

World banners

The first depicts day time, the garden of Eden, the narrow road which leads to heaven (the golden city) and the three crosses on the hill. The second depicts night time, Mount Sinai where Moses received the ten commandments and the golden city (Heaven). Both banners feature a spray painted background and are complete with characters dressed in costumes from around the world.

Praise banners

Made with the children in Sunday School. The background is a double thickness of felt and all shapes are made of felt with added embellishments. The instruments were individually stencilled with gold and silver paint onto felt then mounted on with double sided Velcro to give a raised appearance. Working with banners and with the children has been an absolute pleasure. Often the final result takes me genuinely by surprise as I marvel at what has been achieved by listening to God.

Tricia Lloyd
Bushey Baptist Church
Watford

These banners hang in the church vestibule where they are lit up and can be seen from the road

Easter banner

Celebratory banner

Noah's Ark

This six foot high banner, for a new crèche room at a church, was great fun to make. We used bright colours and a variety of attractive materials and textures for children to touch and easily recognise. Everything was very firmly stitched on!

The grass is fur fabric, the zebras are of patterned crimplene and the ladybirds are buttons. The pig squeaks on pressure. The hippo's mouth opens and closes with a zip to reveal a patterned tongue. The crocodile's mouth opens revealing white teeth and a red velcro tongue. The ostrich's body is a wool pompom. The fish are made of silver ironing board covering. The butterflies are of shimmering material and there are bells on the eaves of the ark. Some of the pairs of animals are obvious and some harder to find.

Joan Waldron and friends, Chandlers Ford United Reformed Church

Taking Part in a Group

The majority of banners described in this book are the product of group work. They bear witness to the friendship, fellowship and fun which can develop as people seek God's Word for their church/community, desiring God's glory to be celebrated.

The diversity of the banners shows the wide range of skills and expertise required from the vision and initial design to completion. There should be room for everyone to be expressive in their faith and in touch with their creativity. Some may begin by cutting out and glueing but they may go on to develop new gifts, even perhaps be the ones to conceive the words or the pictures. Being in a group gives a cross fertilisation of ideas but also provides boundaries within which we can be accountable to one another.

Leading a Group

Some groups manage well without a leader, especially if they are short term in nature and focussed on a special event.

If a group is to be sustained, there are many practical tasks to be undertaken such as responsibility for convening meetings, setting deadlines, communicating with church leaders, attracting new members, overseeing storage and hanging of banners and arranging special events. These tasks may be delegated around the group or one person may emerge as a leader.

A leader will also want to encourage members in their gifting and ensure that people have an opportunity for expression. If there are times of disagreement they will be responsible for arbitration and generally ensure that there is an open, honest and positive atmosphere in which people can work. Underpinning the whole effort in prayer and reliance on the Holy Spirit and providing stimulation, vision, direction and possibly, pastoral care could also be a leader's responsibility.

Advent and Christmas   Pentecost

Seasonal Banners

These banners are two of a set of five that are hung at the front of our church and are changed with the liturgical seasons

Valerie Bennett and Phil Moseley,
Macdonald Road Methodist Church

A design may be best without text if words would say the obvious thing that is clearly stated by the picture. Sometimes it is good if words say something slightly different to the design and so add to the significance of the whole.

The 'I Was' Banner

This represents verses 35, 36 and 40 of Matthew 25. 'For I was hungry and you gave me something to eat, I was thirsty and you gave me something to drink, I was a stranger and you invited me in. I needed clothes and you clothed me, I was sick and you looked after me, I was in prison and you came to visit me...'

'Whatever you did for one of the least of these brothers of mine, you did it for me.'

I am the Light of the World

People of the world come to Jesus as he is lifted up as the Saviour, Lord and Light of the World.

This banner was first used in 1994 when we held a flower festival on the theme 'The Year of the Family' and was placed above the communion table under the title 'The World Family'.

Pentecost Banner

The silhouette of Christ in majesty is superimposed on a dove. The Christ figure is the statue on the summit of Corcovado, overlooking Rio de Janeiro. The banner was inspired by the logo of the World Methodist Council's meetings in Rio in 1996.

The background was made from a fine brocade with grey threads forming a pattern. The dove, clouds and letters were cut from a thin silver coloured material and glued into place.

Ann Matthews, Pat Pritchard and friends – the Methodist Church

Silk Painting

Celebrating the millennium with a new altar cloth and lectern fall, we used silk painting for the first time. We used gold coloured heavy fabric as background. Then we painted a large piece of silk, green, screwed it up and dried it so that a mottled effect was obtained, (We did this outside on the grass on a summer evening!) We cut this fabric into long strips of about 12.7 cm (5 in.) wide and wrote in outline on it in gutta some of the many names of our Lord Jesus, Emmanuel, Saviour, etc. These letters were filled in with gold fabric paint. We then appliquéd these four strips all round the edge (except for the corners) of the altar cloth and bordered them with gold braid.

Next four 18 cm (7 in.) squares of green silk were cut, painted with a gold cross in the centre and folded over 5 inch squares of heavy facing material and stitched. Then they were edged with gold braid and the crosses were decorated with 'jewels'. Lastly these corner pieces were stitched in place.

Onto the centre of the frontal we appliquéd a green silk cross that had also been bound in gold braid and decorated with 'jewels'. On the lectern falls we used the green painted silk to make Alpha and Omega symbols, edged them in gold braid and appliquéd one on to the centre of each fall.

Barbara and Janet sewing the small crosses

This was our second banner made entirely of silk using the traditional gutta resist method. We outlined the design and then filled in the area with iron-fix silk paints.

We now hang this banner on the column next to our font and baptismal ewer whenever a person is baptised in church.

Technical Tips

For the altar frontal border we used habotai 10 silk which was dipped in iron-fix dyes, crumpled up to get the marbled texture and left to dry on the grass. We then used Dupont gutta to do the outline of the words and Lumière gold fabric paint to fill them in.

With the dove design we also used habotai 10 silk, water-based gutta and iron-fix silk paints. Books on silk painting are listed in the resources section.

Sandra Bendall and friends, St Thomas Church, Becontree

Praise Verses

The Lord lives! Praise be to my Rock! Exalted be God my Saviour!
(Psalm 18:46)

Ascribe to the Lord the glory due to his name; worship the Lord in the splen-
dour of his holiness.
(Psalm 29:2)

Great is the Lord and most worthy of praise.
(Psalm 48:1)

Let heaven and earth praise Him – the seas and all that move in them.
(Psalm 69:34)

We, your people, the sheep of your pasture will praise you for ever.
(Psalm 79:13)

Exalt the Lord our God and worship at his footstool; he is holy.
(Psalm 99:5)

Praise the Lord, O my soul; all my inmost being, praise his holy Name. (Psalm
103:1)

From the rising of the sun to the place where it sets, the name of the Lord
is to be praised.
(Psalm 113:3)

Let everything that hath breath praise the Lord.
(Psalm 150:6)

Darwin, Australia

Workshop Banners

Aboriginal people built this banner and background as a backdrop to a drama of Jesus walking on the water. It was made at a workshop led by The Harvest School of Ministry, at Nungalinya College, Darwin.

P. Asher, a member of The Harvest School team made the banner of the lamb in the 23rd Psalm and the Aboriginal people created the background.

Deanshanger, Northamptonshire

I am a self-taught Christian painter and vestment designer who uses the medium of painting to portray the message of Christ.

Jubilee Banner

This banner was painted on canvas using fabric paints and is 3.6m x 2.4m (12 ft x 8 ft). The text over Christ's shoulder is from Isaiah 61. Standing around Christ are the poor, imprisoned, mourning, sad, lonely and starving, depicted in black and grey. As they hear the Good News and meet Christ through others they are transformed into people of vibrant colours themselves.

Acrylic paints mixed with fabric medium go much further than small pots of fabric paint.

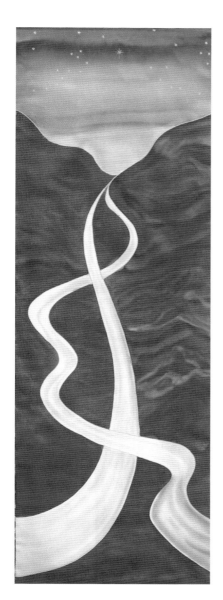

Prepare the Way of the Lord

A purple banner for Advent, painted on silk using steam-fix silk dyes 1.5m x 60 cm (5 ft x 2 ft). The banner can be interpreted in two different ways.

1. John the Baptist crying in the wilderness 'Prepare the way of the Lord, make his paths straight'

2. The road to Bethlehem in Advent and the road to Jerusalem in Lent are both times of journeying and preparation. And which is which? It depends where you are on your journey – they both lead to God.

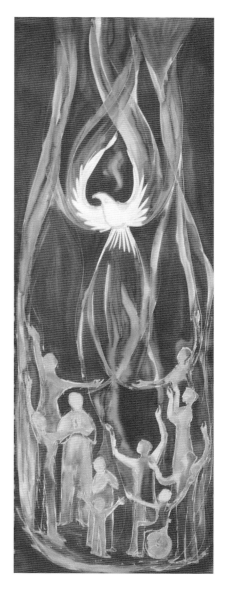

Holy Spirit Banner

Steam-fix dyes on habotai 10 silk, 1.5m x 60 cm (5ft x 2 ft). The Holy Spirit as a dove hovers over a group of people. The banner is painted in shades of reds and yellows. Silk lends itself to colours bleeding into each other so the yellows flicker through the reds and give an interesting impression of flames.

Yvonne Bell
accepts commissions (see Resources)

41

Derby

Juliet Hemingray leads a team of thirteen who make banners and vestments to order. For details see Resources. If you wish to copy any of these designs please first phone Juliet for permission. These three banners were made with Maribou silk paints on painting canvas (from Whaleys – see Resources) and were embellished with embroidery.

Made for St. Richard's Church, Crawley

Made for Army Training Regiment at St. John Moore Barracks in Winchester

He is able to do immeasurably more

This banner was part of a trio we designed and made for our centenary celebrations and reopening of the refurbished church. This particular one speaks of our vision for the future.

This text of Ephesians 3:20 came back to us repeatedly, though we were unsure how to deal with the length of 'immeasurably' from a design point of view, and also the whole verse was too much to fit into the maximum space available.

After a little modification, we went ahead and I'm glad we did because visiting speakers and others frequently refer to this banner and it has been meaningful to so many people.

The design is drawn from the Celtic and Manx connections of the locality. The Celtic cross pattern appears in each of the four corners. The Manx knot pattern, with no beginning and no end, embodies a spiritual concept and can be seen embroidered on the panels surrounding the lettering. This embroidery is more readily appreciated by close inspection. The lettering is basically a contemporary Celtic style. This style of lettering did not contain capitals so we enlarged the word 'He' and stitched a gold cord around the edge to give it emphasis.

The Banner-makers, Broadway Baptist Church

Durres, Albania

Springs of Living Water

The new elders, Viktor and Kristag are being prayed for in the new building of the Disciples' Church, Durres with Pastor Arrid Gogaj.

The banner-makers are a close group of praying women who love making banners. They are very inventive with local materials but also enjoy using ones not available in Albania and sent from friends overseas.

The design is a circle of living waters flowing from a cross. The words are 'He will lead them to springs of living water. God will wipe away every tear from their eyes'. (Revelation 7:17b)

Margaret Gibbs missionary – formerly in Albania now in Asia

Euxton, Chorley, Lancashire

Mother's Union Banner

Following the strong support of Susan Taylor (formerly of Euxton Parish Church), and of the Blackburn Diocesan Needleworkers, Yvonne Downing, a member of the group, designed and made this banner to replace an older one.

The main concerns were to create a banner in sympathy with the simplicity of the building, (hence nothing too glitzy) with full figures of the Mother and Child framed by flowers, including the Christmas rose.

The background fabric is Sanderson's furnishing cotton. The appliqué fabric is polyester Dupion. The lettering fabric is pure silk Dupion.

Appliqué fabrics were first bonded onto light-weight vilene interfacing to stabilise the fabric. Next the shapes were cut out and hand-stitched onto the background fabric. The raw edges were covered with couched stranded cotton. Only the lettering has metal thread outlines couched on. Some fabrics were hand dyed to shade them slightly. The faces, hands and hair were embroidered in a small frame and then applied onto the main frame containing the background material.

The banner was lined with union cotton. The only part that was machine-sewn was the top of the banner where a channel was stitched. This allows the pole which holds the banner to be slotted through and hold the weight. All the rest of the banner was sewn by hand.

The banner was dedicated on Mothering Sunday 2002.

Jesus – Servant King

Created for a series of sermons about Jesus, this banner has figures made from appliquéd cotton fabrics with faces, limbs, cross and lettering in felt. Fabric paint has been used to provide detail, depth and perspective.

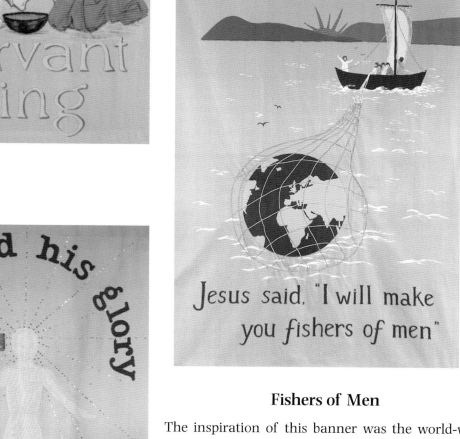

Fishers of Men

The inspiration of this banner was the world-wide mission of the church. The scene is made from coloured felts and the fishing net is knotted string.

The Transfiguration of Christ

The figure of Christ was made from white sheeting with lines of sequins radiating out. Cotton fabrics were used for the disciples and fabric paints provided shape and form.

We want to see Jesus

This banner was first made in paper and fabric for a conference. The message portrayed drew many comments and so we translated it into fabrics.
Raised embroidery and painted faces gave a 3 dimensional effect to the people.

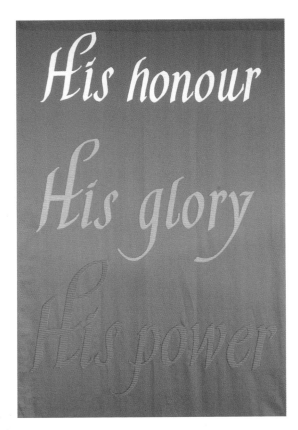

His honour, glory and power

This is the complementary banner to 'We want to see Jesus'. The style of lettering was chosen to convey the message. The increasing size of letters was achieved by photocopying techniques and cut out in felt.

Worship Him

A simple banner using repetitive silhouettes in a variety of colours fading into the background to convey congregational/heavenly worship. The neighbour to this banner features the same silhouettes with 'Praise Him'.

All creatures great and small

One of a pair of banners inspired by the well-known hymn 'All things bright and beautiful' and designed for all ages of the congregation. Coloured felts with embroidered details have been used.

May your loveliness be seen in me

The perfection of God's creation is seen in the world around us. This banner enables children to identify with that. The strong colours of felts have been embellished with a fabric pen to give the detail.

Sheila Barlow and friends – the Baptist Church – the Millmead Centre

The photographer for these banners was Mr Dawson of Dawson Strange Photographers

Happy Valley, Adelaide, South Australia

Happy Valley church of Christ is on the edge of the Adelaide Hills. David Patrick, who has painted over 70 banners, writes 'Isn't it hard to convey the feelings of peace, love, joy, comfort and companionship to be found in knowing our Lord? Some people can do it with wonderful music, others with the right word at the right time, others just seem to radiate God in their personalities. I am none of the above but I like to try through the medium of painting'.

Here is David working in his studio. He writes – The paints used are water-based, low sheen acrylics which I purchase in 1 litre tins. They are intended for sign-writing or feature areas of houses. They are classed as flexible but for low wear use in houses; some of the colours are for indoor use only.

Slightly heavier unbleached cotton calico would be my normal choice for the fabric though I have used cheap single bed sheets and heavy cotton drill. I first seal the fabric with a coat of white acrylic house paint. The edges are hemmed after the painting is finished. A wide hem top and bottom will take the removable poles.

Storage is a major consideration. The paintings are stored, rolled up and placed inside 90 mm (3$^1/2$ in.) diameter PVC storm water pipes, fitted with push on end caps. The tubes are stored lying flat on shelves (better than storage on end). They normally measure 2m x 1.5m (7 ft x 5 ft).

I always paint in my studio, never on site. Whenever possible I use my own photos or my imagination. In some of the banners I have used myself as a model when all else has failed! I don't really know where my ideas come from, my heart or the Holy Spirit, but since the Holy Spirit dwells in my heart maybe it is a team effort of Father and son. I am sustained by the fact that God continues to use me in the ministry.

Painted from Photos

This banner is based on two photos of my own of Aroona Valley in the Flinders Ranges, about 500 km north of Adelaide. The first photo of this normally dry and barren country shows the flush of new growth after early winter rains. The foreground trees and water are from the second photo of a nameless creek somewhere in the same area. The property owners who attempt to make a living from sheep and cattle in this area are well acquainted with hardship and despair; the coming rains and green pasture give them hope to last another year.

I have painted a series of banners based on the 23rd Psalm. I believe the psalmist David must have felt the passion and courage that it takes to live in a dry rugged land and must have experienced the presence of God in the beautiful, lonely majesty of this type of country

Pour Your Spirit

This painting is based on a line from a song (which may be from Psalm 51:10) that we love to sing at Happy Valley. Parts of the creek and rocks are taken from photos stored on a CD. The rest is ideas and feelings evoked by the song. I pray that people seeing a banner like this will experience the presence of the Spirit and uplifting of the heart that I feel when I am painting.

Jesus Sets You Free

When God created us in His image, He made us spiritual beings like Himself, but for a while our spirits are trapped in these frail earthly bodies, caged by earthly desires and needs. I feel as though life is a series of waves, at times I flounder in the troughs, at others it's as though God puts His arm around me and lifts my spirit up like a bird on the wing, and I am free. One day I know I will fly right away from this earth to be with Him always. Then I will truly be free! Come soar with me!

Step Out

The painting was commissioned by this year's president of The Churches of Christ (who is also a member of Happy Valley Church) to illustrate this year's theme – 'Step out of the boat'. The walk on the water happened very early on a stormy morning (Matthew 14:22–33) so I pictured the scene as grey early morning light. It is a very challenging message, particularly here at Happy Valley where we are considering some major changes which will certainly require many of us to 'step out' of our comfortable boat.

David Patrick
Happy Valley Church

53

Pentecost Banners

Birth of a Banner

Ideas and discussions; prayer and panic; despair and delight; stitching and sticking; creativity and self criticism; submitting individual ideas, but reaching a group decision; accepting other people's views, but discerning what God wants us to do; frustration over seemingly endless discussions about colour or design, overtaken by excitement when it actually works; steep learning curves because we keep trying new techniques, and the continual desire to do it better next time; in short, all the joys and problems of working in a Christian banner group!

Maybe a short history of our two Pentecost banners will give you some idea of how it all happens. We spent an afternoon praying and finding out how the Holy Spirit is depicted in the Bible. We read verses where He is pictured in vivid images – fire, wind, water, a dove. He is called a Helper, a Comforter, and Counsellor, an Encourager. He falls on us, fills us, transforms us and purifies us. How much of all this could we include in a banner? What message did we want our banner to convey? We decided to focus on two passages: Acts 2 – the dramatic outpouring of the Holy Spirit on the disciples at Pentecost, depicted by flames of fire and the sound of rushing wind; and Revelation 22 with its picture of the river of life flowing from the throne of God, bringing cleansing, growth, healing and refreshment.

There was general agreement that both banners should contain the symbol of the cross, and some people picked up the Alpha and Omega idea from Revelation, and felt that should be included – God the Holy Spirit is the beginning and the end of all things. Armed with all these ideas and the inspiration of swirling ribbons from a photograph, the design gradually grew. Instead of conventional flame shapes, why not use the ribbon idea, which could easily become flowing water by varying the colour scheme? Simple outlines of people could represent the disciples receiving the Spirit at Pentecost on one banner, and the multitudes of heaven who have 'washed their robes' in the other. The cross would form the basis of the background in both, as the centre of our faith. The Alpha symbol would mark the beginning of the church, and Omega the end of time. The dove, as the most immediately recognisable symbol of the Spirit, would descend on the disciples on the first banner and rise up from the water carrying the leaves of the tree of life on the second. In this way, the designs are similar in form and yet distinct in their message.

Having got the design sorted out, the fun started! We rummaged through all our boxes of fabric and found ourselves, as usual, surrounded by a kaleidoscope of colour and texture. Blues and greens for water were relatively easy, but reds and oranges for flames proved tricky – nothing seemed quite right. The solution was finally inspired by a piece of material which included vivid green, purple and gold combined with red – it fairly 'zinged' with its vibrancy, so conventional orange flames were out and purple and green came in! The people were a problem too – the original idea of 'white robes of heaven' just didn't seem to work and detracted from the white dove, so the solution was to use different shades of net and create a glow from the flames in one and the effect of being 'in' the water in the other.

We pray that our banners will speak to the congregation and help them to meditate and focus their thoughts before and during services. God communicates in many ways and others may find far more meaning in them than was ever conceived by us during their making.

Ruth Cundy and friends, St. Mark's Church, Harrogate

Communion Banners

When our church was re-ordered a few years ago, we realised that the ideal place for banners was on each side of the chancel arch, so since then we have designed our banners in pairs, which gives added scope for developing themes and balancing design and colour. We are also restricted by the width of the pillar, which is only 70 cm (28 in.), so they are all very long and narrow.

These two were designed to be used at any time of year, and their main focus is the cross, with the symbols of Communion closely linked to it. The crown of thorns is associated with the cup of suffering, and is balanced by the crown of glory.

The different motifs were made separately and then stitched by hand onto the background material. The bunches of grapes, ears of corn, and chalice and paten were lightly padded to give depth.

Sent and Serving

In these banners we explored how the shape and layout of words could enhance their meaning. As Jesus sends his disciples into the world, his words are in the shape of the globe, and the fabric used is in shades of blue and green. His claim that the Son of Man came 'not to be served but to serve' makes the shape of a cross, the ultimate act of service. The figures underline the message but are kept deliberately simple and stylised.

The words are all attached by Bondaweb. The figures are lightly quilted to give a little texture, then sewn on, and outlined by couching twisted wool cords around them.

Banner for a Hospice

We were very thrilled to be asked to make banners for the chapel in St. Gemma's Hospice in Leeds, and they took a long time to design and create. Because of the layout of the chapel, and its furnishings, the two banners had to be of different lengths, which was an interesting challenge in itself. We were also aware of the need to make them appropriate and helpful to people of all faiths or none, who were going through a very difficult time. The theme of 'peace' seemed an obvious place to start and we chose some words from the beautiful Celtic prayer 'Deep peace of the flowing air to you...'

The colours had to blend in with the chapel decoration, but we also felt that they should be restful colours which you could sit and look at quietly. All the lines and the words curve and flow.

The background was all sewn by hand (which was very time consuming) and the words applied with Bondaweb.

Banner for Albania

The Baptist Church in Tirana was asked by a prison guard if it was possible to have some bright welcoming banners for a room set aside as a prison chapel. We heard about this request.

We prayed and tried to imagine what it would be like to be confined to prison. We were aware that many prisoners and visitors would have no previous knowledge of Christianity and its symbols. We decided on John 6:37 where Jesus says these words of unconditional acceptance and welcome 'Whoever comes to me, I will never turn away.'

The Baptist pastor in Tirana gave us the correct translation via e-mail. Our design was influenced by a banner from St. John's Church Welling, for which we are very grateful. The multi-coloured figures making their way to the cross seem to echo the words and layers of net were used to highlight the cross and form a misty background.

Banner for Nepal

This banner was made for a small church community in the hills of Nepal. The text is 'Rejoice in the Lord always', an attitude evident in many Nepali Christians in spite of the hardships of everyday life and the difficulties of living out their faith. We made this banner quite small 60 x 35 cm (2 ft x 1 ft 2 in.) and we backed it with heavy plastic to protect it from damp seeping through the rough wall where it would probably hang.

Ruth Cundy and friends
St Mark's Church, Harrogate

An Away-Day Banner

I was invited to talk about 'Banner-making for Beginners' at a church Away-Day at Sutton-on-Derwent, York. The theme was 'Let's worship God together'.

In the morning there were talks on 1) Words for Worship - poetry. 2) Prayer and Praise - intercessions and 3) Banner-Making. In the afternoon there were two hour practical sessions. The aim was to produce contributions for the closing worship service.

Everything was ready for action and the group set to work enthusiastically. Background fabric had been prepared and the edges stitched (no lining). A hanging cord and rod were ready. The wording had been decided 'Let us praise God together'. The group chose from two sets of lettering and templates were provided. Other templates were also ready for 'flowers' and 'people'. We decided on colours. Soon many brightly coloured pieces of felt were ready for use.

The group worked together very well, cutting out, arranging the design and glueing on the pieces with PVA adhesive and were delighted when the banner was ready for the worship service. It was bright and cheerful, the sparkling flower centres shone as they caught the light and the whole effect was simple and positive.

Rachel McHugh and friends – St Mary's Church

One hour banner – for all ages

5 minute introduction on theme – groups of 3-4 discuss briefly
• sketch original designs • draw patterns or use templates (enlarged) • scan Good News Bible and/or other sources.
Completed backgrounds, dowel rods, cords, some materials and glue provided.
Participants bring further materials and scissors.

Adapted from Alec T. Rolls,
Methodist Youth Training Officer

High Wycombe, Buckinghamshire

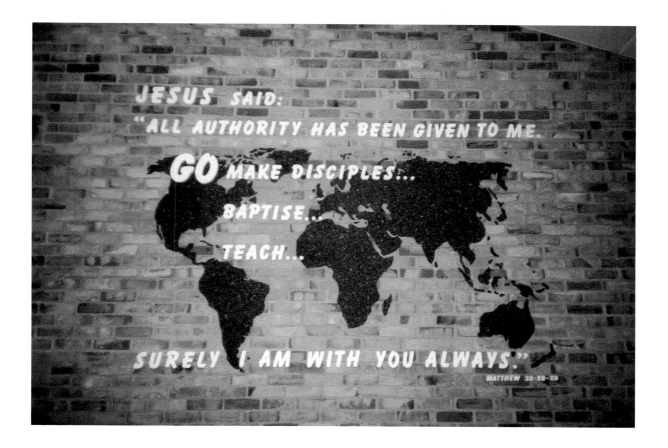

This wall map nearly 3m (10 ft wide) was made by the Pastures Church Banner Group to help the church focus its vision for praying for the whole world.

A précis of the Great Commission from the end of Matthew's Gospel was cut from 2 cm ($^4/_5$ in.) thick polystyrene using a hot wire cutter. It was overlaid on a world map cut from cork tiles mounted on almost invisible net.

The map was fastened to a plain brick wall at one side of the church by a lot of Blu-tak and the minimum number of small wall tacks so that it can be eventually removed with no damage to the wall.

Once in position the net was carefully cut away, just leaving a little for strength around the small islands to keep them in place. We believe that the message was an inspiration for the church's worship during the year that it hung in place.

Rosemary Woodcock and friends
The Pastures Methodist Church, Downley

Kumasi, Ghana

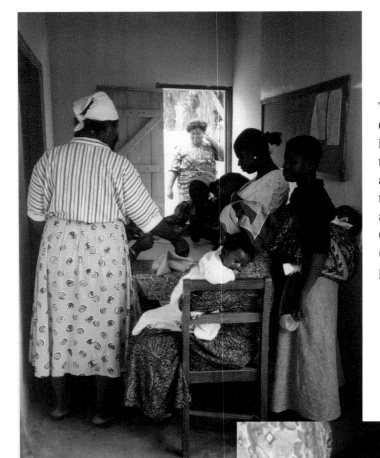

The Women's Leadership Training Retreat in Kumasi

This was organised by the King's Church in Ghana but other ladies were invited to join. There were seminars in the mornings on the theme of the 'I ams'. The banner making took place in the afternoons aided by Jan Lephard and Megan Sainsbury from the King's Church, Prestwood, Buckinghamshire (England) who had brought kits prepared for the theme.

Everyone took part beginning with prayer. Each group worked on one of the 'I ams'. You could see the oneness and unity of each group. There was so much enthusiasm and so much joy. It was wonderful. Each person wanted to take part. This was a new venture but skills quickly came to create these original collage banners. With quick-sticking glue, results were easily obtained and the banners completed in two afternoons.

Each banner was presented with a song, the participants dancing in praise to the Lord for the completion of the banners to his glory.

Julie, Esi, Margaret and Mary with their banner

Each of the women's leaders took one home to the various churches. Getting the idea helped a few of them produce their own in later days.

Mary Odame and friends,
The King's Churches, Kumasi

Jemima, Constance, Janet, Beatrice and Asabere hold their banner

Kwa Zulu Natal, South Africa

The Quilt

Wanting to make a banner celebrating God's creation, with an African theme, suddenly our inspiration came! Gusta, who runs a sewing class, with my help, at an Aids Orphanage and Community Care Centre, decided we would make a small quilt of squares with African images, using fabric paints.

Gusta copied designs from a sheet of wrapping paper onto material and the children each chose and painted one.

Then they added colourful borders. Gusta edged the colours with a black permanent marker. It was all pieced together with navy fabric and looked stunning when at a charity auction it raised R 3000 (approx £220). This was spent on sewing machines and other new materials for our class.

Be Jubilant Africa

We used similar images to the ones on the children's banner. We decorated the sides with 'Ndebele' type patterns. Black felt was cut into the required shape and then individual colours were put underneath. The Ndebele people live north of Johannesburg and have always decorated their houses with these kind of patterns. The words are adapted from Isaiah 65:18 '...rejoice forever in what I will create...' And 'jabulani' means 'be jubilant'. (There is a well-known chorus we sing 'Jabulani Africa'). This banner was made by our minister's wife Carol de Kock and myself. Gusta gave advice.

Marilyn Payne
Hillcrest Presbyterian Church, Greater Durban Area

He is Risen

This was all fabric except the gold which was a mixture of gold braid fabric and glitter. Marilyn writes, 'We are all involved in the design and preparation of the banners and then I do the sewing. I print the letters on the computer and often the ladies in our home group help to cut them out.'

Marilyn Payne and friends

I will pour out my Spirit

The Pentecost banner was made by Gusta Tyrer and Marilyn Payne.

For the background we used photosensitive dye sprinkled with coarse salt. This proved very effective and a hot sunny windless day speeded the drying process. The figure and letters were glued on.

Hillcrest Presbyterian Church,
Greater Durban Area

Lahore, Pakistan

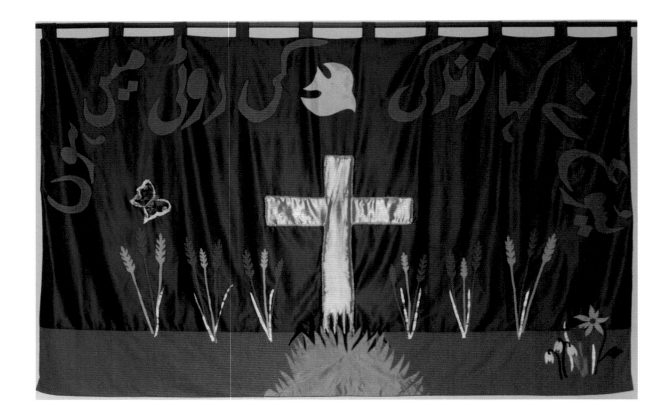

I am the Bread of Life

Eight wives working with Operation Mobilisation, meet once a month, four Pakistani, one Singaporean, one German, one British and one Swedish. A big bare wall in our dining-cum-meeting room had been staring at us for two years. Lacking experience we realised we needed to pray.

Different ideas came to us most of which had to do with food (dining room) or harvest (being a mission). So the Bible verse is, Jesus said 'I am the Bread of Life'.

The wheat symbolises both the harvest to be reaped as well as the food we need. The cross in the middle of the harvest field represents Jesus, the Bread of Life. The butterfly is the symbol of the new birth (and we needed a little splash of colour). One of the brothers came past as were working and insisted on the dove.

My church at home in Guildford sent bondaweb and vilene and these came in very useful, especially for the Urdu letters and the wheat.

Pakistani bazaars are real treasure troves for inexpensive materials, braids, laces and pearls. We used a mixture of silks and cotton and a heavy silky curtain for the background. A gifted brother drew the Urdu lettering free hand and then we decided the size of the banner. It is approximately 2.5m x 1.66m (8 ft 3 in. x 5 ft 5 in.).

Kerstin Wakely and friends, Operation Mobilisation

Botswana Banner

Botswana and Leicester Mothers' Union groups are linked by prayer and when one of the members from Botswana visited in 1989 we were asked to make a banner for the cathedral in Gabarone. We were asked to use certain symbols and a group of us worked sections separately and then the pieces were attached to the banner on the frame. This took about a year.

On the left is the Bishop's badge. On the right is the Mother's Union badge, surrounded by mealies, a staple food.

The Madonna holds the Christ child, whose right hand is raised in blessing, while his left one holds the orb and cross. The acacia tree surrounding them is full of yellow blooms – the Light of Christ and the thorns the symbol of His suffering. The grey lowrie sits on top of the tree, like an angel warning of danger lurking. The blue background represents heaven and Mary's colour, while the sandy colour represents the Kalahari desert.

My husband and I were able to take it to Gabarone and it was presented to the cathedral at a special service in 1990. Much jubilation took place.

Lilian Coates, Leicester Mother's Union

This badge represents Botswana. Cog wheels represent industry, wavy blue bands reliance on water, a bull's head the cattle industry. The zebras and an elephant tusk represent natural fauna and a head of sorghum represents agriculture. Pula means rain.

Little Budworth, Cheshire

Millennium Altar Frontal Project

The original inspiration was from colours in the East window of St. Peter's, Little Budworth, (much loved by the parishioners) and a church window in France seen on a cycling tour.

After a paper model had been approved by the Parochial Church Council, silk pieces and instructions were sent out to nearly 100 people – many in the parish, others in the U.S.A., France and Germany as well as other parts of the U.K. The age range varied from 6–90 years. The plan was that each person should embroider on the Vilene their name, address and a text or words which would then be hidden for posterity behind the silk piece.

The kit contained needle, sewing cotton that matched the silk piece (wound on a card); embroidery thread (also matching); pelmet Vilene pre-cut in diamond shape with a pre-drawn margin of 1.5 cm (3/5 in.) and pre-cut silk diamond 1 cm (2/5 in.) larger with a 7 mm (3/10 in.) border of bondaweb already ironed on. We included a stamped addressed envelope.

The instructions were:

1. Write your name, brief address and/or a text or dedication or what you wish, in pencil in the centre of the Vilene diamond.

2. Over-sew the writing with any colour of sewing cotton in hand or machine stitch – legibly!

3. Cover the other side of the Vilene diamond with the pre-cut silk piece making sure the turnings have the bondaweb (adhesive) on the inside. Do not iron the bondaweb.

4. Turn over the edges and then pin the sharp points first. Then pin the opposite sides.

5. Stitch, using matching sewing cotton (on card) going only partly through the Vilene so the stitches don't show on the front.

6. Stitch all the way round, making sure that the points at the top and bottom of the diamond are sharp (finished size 22.75–23 cm [9 in.]). Next embroider along the front edge about $1/2$ cm ($1/5$ in.) from the edge. Using running stitch, any straight stitch or any embroidery pattern (optional but not too heavy). If you hand-stitch please use the embroidery thread.

7. Please return within 6 weeks in the SAE.

I hand-stitched each completed diamond separately onto a pre-drawn purple, fireproof linen background grid. Half-diamond shaped edge pieces were made and added. Padded gold kid lettering was used for the cross in the centre and the text above.

In all my work, prayer and the needs of the parish or community are paramount, and a full-scale paper model must be fully approved before I start. In my file on this frontal Celtic writings and the meditations of medieval mystics appear – these were an encouragement to me when doubts arose. My husband, John, is a great support to my work.

Two church windows and the advent theme of renewal, rebirth and rekindling the light helped to inspire the frontal. As well as celebrating Advent it symbolises the coming together of our different forms of worship, personalities, rituals and traditions through our belief in our one Lord.

The hardest thing is to wait for the design to evolve and I am often surprised by the inspiration which can come at any time. It has been a tremendous privilege to use what talent I have to promote our life in Christ. The gift for me is that, after completion, there is always an added extra dimension to the work – surely the gift of the Holy Spirit – albeit there has been much journeying and agony along the way. It is always a surprise, sometimes a shock, unexpected and even humbling, a reminder that I was not alone in creating the project

Planned, designed and assembled by Andrea Higginson,
helped by 100 people!
Andrea is now living in France

Livingstone, Zambia

A Church in a Marquee

We are based in Southern Zambia in a town called Livingstone (famous for the Victoria Falls, named by Dr. David Livingstone) 10 km from the Zimbabwe border. The Covenant Life Church, to which the ladies belong, meet in a marquee where the banners are proudly displayed.

The 12 ladies in the group prayed about the designs to use and worked in groups of four, although they did change round a little. The fabric backing for the 'Go and make disciples' was purchased locally as it is a chitenge – the cloth that women traditionally wrap round their waists to act as skirts. I helped by measuring, cutting and positioning the pieces. They did the rest.

The standing frames were made by a local carpenter as it is difficult to hang things on the walls of the marquee.

Christine Crowther, Covenant Life Church

Lettering

In many of the banners displayed in this book the words are the central focus. This reflects the value attached to the Word of God and the power it brings.

Finding the best type of font with its size, shape and colour and the positioning of the words is an important task. It has been made easier in recent years with so many groups having access to a computer. This can open up a huge variety of fonts which can be adapted for each occasion, whether celebratory, solemn, direct, formal, etc. They can be printed out to the exact size required ensuring accuracy and speed. Many groups build up sets of their favourite letters and have a library that can be used over and over again.

At times the formal and uniform effect of the lettering can be discordant with the theme of a banner which may be about freedom and spontaneity. A more individual and manual approach may be needed (see banners from Kumasi, Ghana and Livingstone, Zambia). Other times, lettering will be required to fit into odd shapes and unusual spaces and again, a hand-drawn approach will be preferable.

Observation of lettering in newspapers, magazines, shop name-boards and books can show the effects and impact of different approaches. A photocopier can be used to enlarge the chosen lettering to the required size.

Once the letters are cut out in paper they can be placed front side down on the back of the chosen non-fray material, attached either by sellotape or pins and then cut out and glued or sewn onto the banner.

Using sticky back felt, still only available in limited colours, or iron-on Vilene and Bondaweb, the whole process can be made much easier.

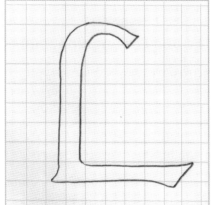

Alternatively, cord can be couched directly onto the banner to provide a flowing effect, or embroidery stitches, machine or hand-sewn, can be used directly onto the banner or in conjunction with the cut-out letters. Sometimes calligraphy can be chosen which is started by enlarging and decorating the initial letter.

See the banners by Princes Risborough Baptist Church

Harvest and Communion Banners

Our Task To make a pair of 3-dimensional banners, approximately 2.4m x 2.1m (8 ft by 7 ft), for the main auditorium of Stopsley Baptist Church, Luton.

Our Verse 'As long as the earth endures...seedtime and harvest will never cease'. (Genesis 3:22)

As you can see from the photos we combined the thanksgiving of harvest with the celebration of Holy Communion, thus extending the time the banners could be displayed.

The Challenge To create a 3D effect on two large banners, without making them too heavy.

The Solutions

Wadding was suitable for the smaller areas but for the larger ones (i.e. the sack of corn and the bread) we used bubble plastic that worked very well. The grain falling from the sack was made by 'hooking' fabric through the sacking. The leaves, glass, bread and breadboard were fabric-painted onto cotton sheeting and then appliquéd onto the background. The wheat was made with muslin, and parts of the leaves were quilted to make them stiffer and therefore able to stand out. We mounted them onto well-constructed, wooden frames.

Jane Butler and friends, Stopsley Baptist Church

Luxembourg

Fabric Paint Banners

We decided to find an activity to involve our teens in the church and chose as our theme the names of God. The teens were encouraged to try different textures and also to think carefully of the colours they would use to illustrate a name. In this banner the idea of the 'beginning and end' was conveyed by the symbols of the sun and moon and the shading of blue from light to dark.

The banners are made of unbleached calico-curtain lining and the medium used was fabric paint. This was applied with sponges on the larger surfaces and brushes for the finer artwork.

The children in our church were eager to paint. We chose the theme of creation. We wanted one that had various aspects and pictures ranging from simple to more detailed. This banner grew step by step with no preconceived plan.

Basically they used the same materials and methods as the teenagers. The animals were out-lined with stencils. The pictures were sewn onto a larger thicker fabric and the wording done with several layers of silver fabric paint.

Jessica Mills & friends, Oasis Church of God

74

'The Open Door' (Revelation 3:8)

The Apostle John sends the message of Jesus to the church at Philadelphia assuring them that through the death and resurrection of Jesus there is, for all time, a way back to God.

We look beyond the threshold of the open doorway and see the risen Lord Jesus waiting and ready to be with us always. The cross is a reminder of our salvation and also of our personal cross as we follow him. The star at the entrance is the Morning Star (Rev. 2:28), the Lord himself, who lights the path across rough ground to heaven itself.

'He Will Come' (Hosea 6:3)

This banner was hung when Marcham was experiencing a particularly lovely early spring with crisp, sunny mornings and welcome light rain. Sun and rain in due season were crucial in Hosea's day and suggest God's utter dependability. The words encouraged us with a reminder of His faithfulness.

'Press on' – bright colours on black symbolised light in dark places.

'He will come' – letters mounted on gold to reflect the padded gold fabric sun.

'As surely as' – letters placed to suggest movement of the sea.

'Spring rain' – sequins of green and blue on fine gold thread falling on fertile ground of 3D flowers and greenery.

Judith Adderley and friends, All Saints Church

Easter Banners

We used a combination of methods. In the early days we mostly used the overhead projector, taping a large sheet of butchers' paper, the size of the banner, to the wall and tracing over the outline. This was how we did the lettering for the Easter banners.

As we learnt to use computers we composed the lettering on them, then photocopied and enlarged. Alternatively we used the overhead projector which is good for getting the size right and seeing the whole picture.

The musical notes were added after the banners were hung and really brought them to life.

Christmas Banners

There were three of us in our group, Barbara, Joy and myself. Barb struggled with cancer but even when really ill worked on determinedly, finding release and satisfaction in her achievement. She is now with the Lord but her work lives on – an encouragement to her church family.

All banners have been made using the no sew appliqué technique and the edges sealed with dimensional fabric paint. Most of our banners are made on sample pieces of rubber backed curtain material. The plastic rod ends are sprayed with gold paint

In these complementary Christmas banners, iridescent plastic stars highlight the Southern Cross shining over the community of shops, high rise flats and houses surrounding our church building.

Valerie Main and friends, Mundalla & Brooklyn Park Churches of Christ

Our Saviour's Lutheran Church is located in the rural township of New Hope. With much prayer, faith and exuberance we embarked on praising the Lord through making banners. This banner, made for Epiphany is mostly of felt. The star is covered with metallic paper.

The 'Give Thanks' banner was made for Thanksgiving. The table design is embossed with cotton batting (wadding) giving a 3-D effect. Most of the banners are worked on felt; occasionally we use burlap for a more rustic design.

Barb Winrich and Peggy Kocher

Easter

This small Easter banner with its visual impact and instant message we feel to be ideal in an age when people may not have time or desire to read the gospels. It may arrest attention and give people food for thought. Our banner group was greatly encouraged by contact with other groups around.

The city of Jerusalem is created with fabric paint and fabric pens. The cross was made with thin gold metallic dress fabric which wouldn't take glue. The fabric was cut to shape, hand sewn onto the black felt and then edged by machine. The felt was then trimmed and hand-sewn onto the background.

Elizabeth Redmond and friends
St Bartholomew's Catholic Church

Sunrise

Thinking Him dead,
They prepared their offering,
For a fragrant memory.

Thinking Him dead,
They acted in obedience,
Keeping Sabbat.

Thinking Him dead,
They rose before dawn,
To honour Him.

Thinking Him dead,
They sought His resting-place,
For the last time.

Thinking Him dead,
They recoiled from the light,
Hiding their faces.

Grief-stricken, desolate, troubled,
  confused, afraid.

And then – an Angel!
'Fear not. Remember, He told you.'

Then they recalled His words;
And with the daybreak
Shattering their weary hopelessness,

Deep within their hearts,
JOY exploded.
        He's Alive.

Ruth Wood

Water Hanging

This was created, using paint, wax resist, stencil and spray paint, for the college chapel of Wycliffe Hall, Oxford. The banner is designed in five panels to hang from one rod, echoing the five windows.

It was created by the Rev. Val Turner (ex-student, right picture) and hung there during 2000 and 2001. It was re-hung for the Summer School of 2003 providing an appropriate background for its theme of 'Creation and Creativity'. During the Summer School some of the delegates made a collage under her guidance

Paris, France

March for Jesus

These photos were contributed by Jacques Barbero who is the honorary president of the French March for Jesus Movement. Marches were held in many countries around the world in the 1990s and in 2000. Graham Kendrick composed the songs and music. There was a focus for prayer during the marches in 1998 for the suffering church and in 2000 for the world's children.

The book 'Banners around the World' encouraged people not only to make triumphant banners but also some that expressed God's love for those in need. Examples were 'He cares for you', 'Jesus mends broken lives', 'His body broken for you' and 'Jesus our Provider'.

The Meaning of Colour

Yellow is the symbol of the sun. It is the colour of promise, the future, heaven, joy and celebration.

Orange suggests fire and energy.

Red often gives life to a picture. It suggests vitality and movement, love and danger. It can represent the passion and death of Christ and is the colour of atonement and sacrifice. It is also the colour that represents the season of Pentecost.

Purple is the colour traditionally worn by kings and rulers and represents the majesty of Christ. It also represents the seasons of Advent and Lent, times of penitence and preparation for Christmas and Easter.

Blue has a tendency to recede and is a cool colour. It is the sky colour, the colour of the heavens and speaks of the infinite, eternal nature of the divine Son of God. It is also used to represent Mary, his mother.

Green is the colour of nature and symbolises growth and hope. Like blue it has a calming effect and is refreshing; it speaks of life and renewal, of everyday times and represents the season of Trinity, the season between Pentecost and Advent.

White suggests forgiveness, purity, joy, celebration and glory. Christ was wearing white when He was transfigured on the mountain.

Brown is a combination of colours. It represents the earth and the autumn of the year.

Black is the absence of colour. It is used to represent sin and death but in ancient Egypt it was the colour of the Resurrection. Some people find large areas of it depressing.

Gold is symbolic of divine righteousness. It speaks of celebration, kingship and majesty, glory and heaven.

Father, Son and Holy Spirit
Dovegate Prison Chapel, Staffordshire

A prison chaplain at Dovegate Prison, previously a priest at St. Ninian's Episcopal Church, Prestwick, which I attended, requested me to design banners for the prison chapel. Each was hung temporarily in St. Ninian's and blessed before being sent. Many people contributed materials and it felt as if they were sending their greetings to the prisoners.

The sky background of 'Father, Son and Holy Spirit' is hand-dyed cheesecloth (to represent heaven, eternity and sky). The hands are made of layers of linen and canvas, lightly quilted. The dove is made of satins and layers of sheer fabrics, again lightly quilted. The nails and crown of thorns are made of silk, velvet, sheer fabrics and gold lamé. A variety of threads (some of glitter) were used in sewing. Satin stitch (close zig-zag) was used to apply the layers to each other and ultimately to the backing material. Borders were reinforced with pelmet stiffening and applied last of all. Fabric sleeves were sewn on the reverse side for handling poles.

Come Follow Me

The brief was to design Bible scenes without text so that people could ask their own questions and let the images speak to them. High security meant we had limited access for measuring and the unusual shape of the chapel was a real challenge.

A similar method was used as in 'Father, Son and Holy Spirit'. Large areas of land, hills and water were applied first and the hills were lightly quilted. Figures, boats and fish were constructed separately and then applied; some of these fabrics were backed with iron-on facing (Vilene) to avoid fraying. A similar diversity of fabric types was used including cottons, linens, silks, sheers, lamés and netting. The finishing process was the same.

Do You Truly Love Me?

Again fabrics were laid out and layered over lining backing. Water areas, sand and cliffs were applied first and the foreground was lightly quilted. Figures, boat, bread, fire and fish were constructed separately and then added to background. If I was unsure of colour ideas, colour combinations or sewing techniques, I made up samplers before a final decision. Again I used a similar range of materials and the same finishing and border technique were used.

Design Details of All Three Banners

In each case the colour design was made into a line drawing which was photocopied onto an acetate for use with an overhead projector. The image was then projected onto the wall and a full-size scale drawing was made on wall-paper lining paper which then served as a cartoon for placing pieces of material onto while constructing each banner, and also as a base to trace off pattern pieces. Each banner was drawn on curtain lining material, padded with 'quilting liner' and individual layers of colour were built on this base – applied mostly with machine stitching with some hand sewing.

Melitta Bosworth, and associated with St. Ninian's Church, Prestwick
and St Matthews Church Kilmarnock, and now at the Bield Retreat Centre near Perth.
(available for help – see resources)

Sing to the Lord

This was created to decorate a balcony above the organ and piano – hence its elongated shape. As there were many words we decided an illuminated lettering for the three capitals, using a consider-able amount of appliqué and embroidery around them. The banner took about eleven months to make and had to be mounted on a wooden frame to support its length.

Come Holy Spirit

This banner signifies the Holy Spirit coming with fire. Each flame is individually shaped from rich lurex fabrics in copper, red and gold. Red satin appears in the flames which are each beaded to create brightness and a shimmering effect.

Much embroidery on the dove makes the bird seem very real and its black bead eyes seem to look straight at you. People have commented that it seems to fly out toward them!

Harvest Banner

This was a challenge. We wanted to include a rich variety of God's creation and yet not overcrowd the banner. The other aim was to make everything look real.

Our starting point was the large poppy – its centre black beads and its petals crimson satin. The style of the foliage and petals is after William Morris, who relied simply on shape and colour to suggest what objects were. To avoid a cluttered look we used several plain fabrics and kept the colour palette to a minimum.

Ann Trollope and Alison Watts
Princes Risborough Baptist Church

Princes Risborough, Buckinghamshire

The Lord is our Shepherd

The banner was designed for the back of our church piano which is situated next to where the Sunday School are seated. We wanted to include the children as much as possible in its creation, so that they could take ownership of it, and also feel a sense of belonging in the church family.

Each child had the chance to design their own face. Of course help was given to the little ones! The faces were then arranged in height order on the banner. We even had to add a new person as he was born just before the banner was finished. We hope children will enjoy looking at it for many years to come.

Nicola Hirst – The Baptist Church

This is a collage banner – other suggestions are:
1. Using fabric paints to make prints of hands, feet, leaves etc.
2. Drawing with fabric crayons or fabric painting felt pens on material and applying the pictures to the background with adhesive or stitching.
3. Sticky-backed felt is very handy and comes in a limited range of colours.

A few of the Names and Titles of Jesus in the Bible

- *Alpha (Revelation 22:13); Advocate (1 John 2:1)*

- *Beloved Son (Matthew 3:17); Bread of Life (John 6:48); Bright Morning Star (Revelation 22:16)*

- *Christ (Matthew 16:16)– Chief Cornerstone (Ephesians 2:20)*

- *Door of the sheep (John 10:7)*

- *Emmanuel (Matthew 1:23); Eternal Life (1 John 5:20)*

- *Friend of sinners (Luke 7:34); Faithful and True (Revelation 19:11)*

- *Good Shepherd (John 10:11)*

- *Holy One (Acts 2:27); High Priest (Hebrews 4:14); Hope of Glory (Colossians 1:27)*

- *I Am (John 8:58); Intercessor (Hebrews 7:25)*

- *Jesus (Matthew 1:21) – Judge of the Living and the Dead (Acts 10:42)*

- *King of Kings (Revelation 19:16)*

- *Lamb of God (John 1:29); Lord of Lords (Revelation 9:16); Light of the World (John 8:12)*

- *Messiah (John 1:41); Mediator (1 Timothy 2:5); Man of Sorrows (Isaiah 53:3)*

- *Nazarene (Matthew 2:23)*

- *Only begotten Son (1 John 4:9)*

- *Prince of Peace (Isaiah 9:6)*

- *Ransom (1 Timothy 2:6)*

- *Saviour (Titus 2:13); Son of God (Matthew 4:3); Servant (Isaiah 52:13)*

- *The Truth (John 14:6); Teacher from God (John 3:2)*

- *Unspeakable gift (2 Corinthians 9:15); Unknown God (Acts 17:23)*

- *Vine (John 15:1)*

- *Word (John 1:1); Way (John 14:6); Wisdom of God (1 Corinthians 1:24)*

- *X – Cross-bearer (John 19:17)*

- *Young child (Matthew 2:13); Yes of God (2 Corinthians 1:18–20)*

- *Omega (Revelation 22:13)*

These names are drawn from several different versions of the Bible; some are illustrated in this book

Quinton, Birmingham

Step by Step Inspiration

Here in St. Boniface Church (photo on opposite page) we spend time praying and waiting on God concerning the theme and content of the banners. Having discerned the scriptures we are to illustrate, we begin to work and from time to time will stop and ask God to inspire us for the next stage concerning the details. We find that approaching the work without a completed overall design encourages a truly corporate end result in which God can use our various gifts (those known and not yet known) to achieve a united expression of worship.

The 'I Am' Banners

These are two of a series of six banners. They were made by about ten people working together. They hang on the perimeter wall of our church.

The two longer ones that hang at the front (see the picture opposite) 'I am Alpha' and 'I am Omega' – were made later.

In Birmingham we have easy access to many sources of decorative materials with shops catering for the needs of people making 'saris'

Mary Brown, Maureen Stand and friends

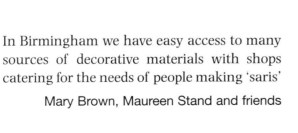

91

Salisbury, Wiltshire

Paper Banners at St. Marks Church

The first banner was made for Advent 1999 on a notice screen. It was a new venture for the church and the letters were made of paper and wrapping foil. This way, had the congregation not been happy, we would not have gone to any great expense.

The following year more banners were made to celebrate the church centenary. This time a clever friend had fixed up hooks at the top of the columns, with a loop of fishing line for hoisting them. The building is enormous and the main banners are 2m (6 ft. 8 in.) long, apart from a small one 1m (3 ft 4 in.) near the door, to greet people. They are made of wallpaper (vinyl is by far the most durable), with letters and motifs stuck on with Blutak. Another large one hangs near the chancel steps. This is made of loop nylon with letters and pictures fixed on with velcro. The backgrounds are royal blue and old gold. More recently I have started using P.V.C. tablecloth fabric for backgrounds, and attached letters with Blutak.

Many of the letters are made of heavy-duty cartridge papers outlined with a fat gold/silver felt pen. I always buy the same type of papers so that the letters are interchangeable. I have built up 'banks' of letters in some styles.

Other letters are made of a wide variety of gift-wrap, foil, pearlised, mottled, lustre and holographic paper. There are so many wonderful textures and colours that it is possible to produce some exciting effects. It is good to write the Lord's name in gold or placed on a reflective surface.

Some members of the congregation find the liturgical colours helpful so I try to include them appropriately. We need a number of banners to make an impact in our large building so I make them on a theme.

Dianne Hollow, St. Marks
with some help from friends

The advantages of paper banners are that they are inexpensive, easily assembled and can help to fill large spaces. They also provide for immediacy of ideas and words. A wonderful variety of paper can be used.

The disadvantages are they are not made to last and also wallpaper as a background isn't very wide.

In Yvonne Coppock's book 'Prepare the Way with Posters' (see resources) there is helpful information on the use of paper. See the index of her book.

Christmas Banners

These two were made for Christmas. The letter style matches although the colours and sizes vary according to word lengths and background.

On the looped nylon banner I have recycled holographic stars from a previous Christmas.

The straw is made of a variety of scraps of gold wrapping paper, some matt, some shiny, sparkly etc. I worked from the outside inwards, breaking up the types of paper and measuring with the cut out baby to make sure I'd covered enough of the cartridge base. None of the pieces are stuck right down, so they give texture.

The baby in the straw is outlined in gold on white cartridge paper and fixed on with Blutak. I put the Blutak pieces around the edges and squidged them towards the middle from his sides, so that he is not flat.
Some of the bright bits catch the light especially the 'straw' nearest the baby is all shiny gold.

'Worship His Majesty' is made with foil and wrapping paper stuck on vinyl wallpaper with Blutak.

93

Easter Banners

The central banner has a looped nylon background. The other two are wallpaper.

Foil mounted on cartridge paper was used. The foil letters were cut out, stuck on and then cut out again leaving a white edge. This helps to give contrast. The silk flowers were put on with safety pins.

With the two paper banners the letter style is the same but the sizes vary according to the length of the longest word/number of words. The flowers here were attached with Blutak for individual blooms and leaves.

The Lord Beside Us

These pictures are three of a set of twelve and show the Lord beside us at different stages and times of our lives. Pictures leave us free to receive from the Lord what He wants to say to us.

The background colour is blue as these banners were made for our Lady Chapel and the material is P.V.C. tablecloth fabric.

I first drew the figures rough on A4 paper and enlarged them on a photocopier to heavy duty cartridge paper. The figures were outlined in a thick indigo Aquarelle stick – Faber-Castel – and attached with Blutak.

Dianne created these figures herself. If you need help with figure-drawing the Good News Bible is a great source. Permission to copy will be freely given. See address at very beginning of this book.

This banner 1 yard 3" x 2 yards 6" (1 x 2 metres) was originally created for Pentecost to hang on the right-hand side of the chancel arch. Four small banners usually accompany it and are hung on pillars in the nave.

I felt the words needed dynamic and arresting lettering to convey the Spirit's power. They are designed in a random way to fit and flow together.

Love, joy and peace we made quite large as they are the ones mentioned first (Galatians 5 v 22, 23). The colours were chosen to reflect their qualities - Love - red foil; Joy - bright orange; Peace - gold foil. The other words are cut out of textured foil, reflecting the light and giving life and sparkle. The dove is white card edged with gold pen.

The background is made of UPVC tablecloth fabric with a matt finish and the letters are attached with Blu-tak.

The design was drawn fairly small and enlarged on a photocopier. The resulting sections were sellotaped together on the floor and the words cut out and arranged on the background. Next the letters were cut as paper patterns for the colourful papers.

The banners at St Mark's which began rather tentatively, have been well received and have become very much a part of things.

Diane Hollow

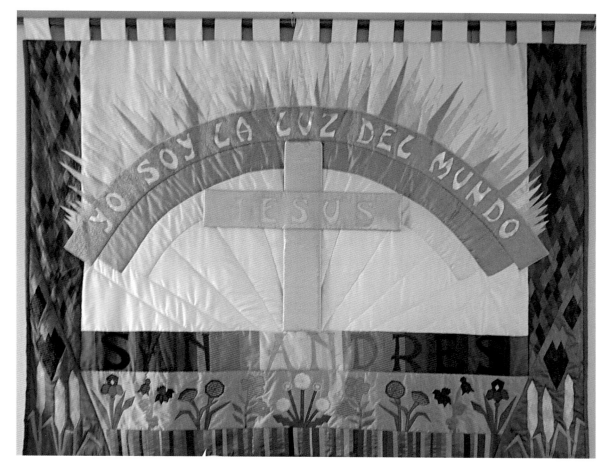

I am the Light of the World

The church is San Andrés in the district of La Reina, Santiago.

When visiting the new building in 1997, Dorothy Sharman from Rutland, England, decided she would like to make a hanging. After sketching ideas and discussing them with Patricio Browne and Tracy Leatherbee, the verse and design were agreed.

The hanging incorporates the Cross; the text 'I am the Light of the World' attached to a curved shape (taken from the design of the wall light fixtures) with rays of light shining upwards and stylised wheat, grapes and flowers representing the following:

> Corn – bread, the Body of Christ
> Grapes – wine, the Blood of Christ
> Dandelion – the symbol of the Passion
> Columbine – the dove, the Holy Spirit
> Iris – the sorrow of the Virgin
> Lily – the purity of the Virgin
> Carnation – pure love

Canon John Cobb and Dorothy Sharman, his mother

The Colours of the Precious Stones in the wall of the Holy City

One of the seven angels...carried me away in the Spirit to a mountain great and high and showed me the Holy City, Jerusalem, coming down out of heaven from God. It shone with the glory of God and it's brilliance was like that of a very precious jewel – like a jasper, clear as crystal. (Revelation 21:9–11)

The wall was made of jasper and the city of pure gold as pure as glass. The foundations of the city walls were decorated with every kind of precious stone. (Revelation 21:18–19)

These are the stones mentioned:

- *Jasper: dark opaque green*
- *Sapphire: pale blue to deep indigo*
- *Chalcedony: usually bluish white*
- *Emerald: bright green*
- *Sardonyx: light to dark brown*
- *Carnelian: red*

- *Chrysolite: bright yellow*
- *Beryl: pale blue-green*
- *Topaz: transparent green*
- *Chrysoprase: bright apple green*
- *Jacinth: reddish orange*
- *Amethyst: violet*

The twelve gates were twelve pearls, each gate made of a single pearl. The street of the city was of pure gold like transparent glass. (Revelation 21:21)

The city does not need the sun or the moon to shine on it for the glory of God gives it light and the Lamb is it's lamp. (Revelation 21:23)

All Things Bright and Beautiful

St. Andrew's United Church is situated in Sault Ste Marie (pronounced Sue Saint Maree), a city of about 72,000 situated at the hub of the Great Lakes at the Eastern end of Lake Superior.

In the spring of 1994, the church's Fellowship Club commissioned Jane Turgeon to make a quilt/wall hanging to fill the 2-storey wall-space beside the new elevator. To make it a congregation-wide project, an invitation was issued to the congregation to make fabric pictures or representations based on the words of the hymn 'All Things Bright and Beautiful'. Each was to be 32 cm ($12^1/2$ in.) square with unfinished edges. Over 35 men, women and children participated. The quilt has crocheted motifs, woven rainbow ribbons, yoyo and button flowers, a yarn rug-hooked tree, a needlepoint cardinal, crewel embroidered Canada geese, cross-stitch flowers, appliqué, pieced work, beads, stones, etc.

In designing the layout, a free-form edge was used to accommodate however many squares were brought in. Catherine Hugill & Jane Turgeon spent a lovely afternoon working out the layout that generally follows sky, earth and water, top to bottom. There is no batting, but after the top group of squares was assembled, and likewise for the rest, they were stitched to a backing of pillow ticking for support. It is approximately 4.2m x 2.1m (14 ft x 7 ft). Reverend Phil Miller attached a large timber batten to the wall and a band of extra-strength wide Velcro is holding the quilt to this.

Praise Banners

Positive words of acclamation were chosen that would encourage our worship. The banners were designed to fit the shape of the columns in the main sanctuary of the church building.

Strong vibrant colours enhanced the boldness of the words. The green cotton material used for a background of one banner, forms the lettering of another and so with the pink, purple and yellow colours. The material was cotton stiffened with a lining of vilene.

Rosas Mitchell and friends, Murray Place Baptist Church

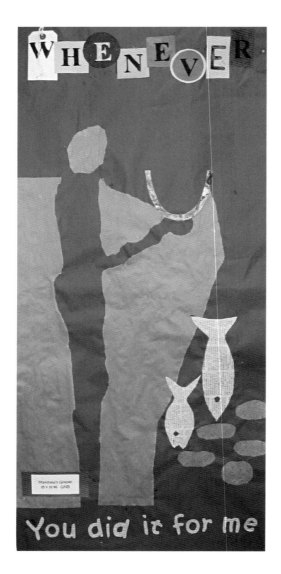 

Mission Posters
Matthew 25:31–46

The designs for the six posters on display for mission's month in the church originated at the time of the Make Poverty History campaign and the G8 summit at Gleneagles July 2005.

The two phrases used from the passage in Matthew are 'whenever' and 'you did it for me'. They are taken from the verse 'whenever you did this for one of the least important of these brothers of mine, you did it for me' translated in the Good News Bible. Jesus is referring to the hungry, the thirsty, the stranger, the naked, those sick and those in prison. Each image on the posters correlates with these different vulnerable groups. Four of these are portrayed here.

You may notice that there are many features that remind us of the challenge of our global world:

- They are made of paper, flimsy and easily disposable
- They all have the same materials but each one is uniquely different
- The figures are simple and could come from any nationality or race and be male or female, young or old
- The materials come from all over the world; newsprint in Chinese, Ukrainian and Arabic; bark cloth, banana plant and handmade paper from Uganda
- Much of the design is made through tearing brown paper, a process over which you have little control and little idea of how things will turn out (PVA glue was used)
- All six posters cost less than five pounds but were costly in terms of time, labour and emotional involvement

Rosas Mitchell & Liz Watt

Made for a home

Created as a gift for the minister and his wife when they retired.

Rosas Mitchell and friend
Murray Place Baptist Church
By kind permission
Rev. Jim and Helen Taylor

Wedding Banner

This was created for my wind-surfing son and his wife! The inspiration came from a painting found by Rosas in a library book. She 'painted' the water in fabrics while I cut out the more geometric windsurf sails. (In 1997 these were all varied and bright colours. Now windsurf sails are all transparent). All pieces were attached to the background with bondaweb and oversewn with a simple zig-zag stitch.

Anne Dreyer and Rosas Mitchell

104

Small Cross Stitch Banners

These small banners 28 cm x 12 cm (11 in. x 4.7 in.) were created and used as gifts to be displayed in the home. Enid's vision is to have small groups of older friends and neighbours meeting to make such cross-stitch items and to share companionship, friendship and fellowship and draw all into a closer relationship with our Lord.

Enid writes – Banners are a rallying point 'We will lift up our banners in the Name of our God' (Psalm 20:5) for He has promised we 'will still bring forth fruit in old age, we will be fresh and green' (Psalm 92:14). She points out that, even with physical restrictions, small banners using words of Scripture can be made to the glory of God. She adds that writing with a needle and thread is easy and many cross stitch magazines print alphabet patterns which can be drawn out on ordinary graph paper.

Materials used – (obtainable by post or from your local needlework shop) are 14 or 11 count Aida cloth, stranded cottons, tapestry needles, bell pull ends, scissors, a graph book and a few monthly cross stitch magazines.

Enid Grantham, Pontygwydr Baptist Church

Easter

Pentecost

At the Rector's request, Jean Hewlett designed these four banners. Others in the church helped to make them. Varying colours of brocade were used for the background.

Margaret Edwards, St. Teilo's Church, Bishopston

Harvest

Christmas

Easter Sunday and Easter Wedding Banners

These were prepared to match the colour scheme and flowers chosen by the bride – gold and ivory – with green leaves added to represent our church.

On the left of the platform we hung the Easter banner. Gold ribbons formed the Cross on which ivy-shaped leaves were entwined reminding us that it was for us that Christ died. Golden yellow daffodils replace a crown of thorns and Easter eggs and chicks illustrate new life found in our risen Saviour.

On the right-hand side we hung the Wedding Banner. By using an assortment of gold ribbons, organza, lamé and satins, we wanted to show love as two become one with interlocking wedding rings; candles indicate two lives burning and working together. Roses represent the ups and downs of life but the Cross of our Lord Jesus Christ is there in the centre of everything reassuring us of His unfailing love.

Beryl Gray, Greenleaf Road Baptist Church

A Caring Church

This banner around the gallery tells the story of Greenleaf Road Baptist Church in about 10m (33 ft 5 in.) of fabric collage. It was made to portray the different areas of ministry in the church.

House and Bible
Study groups
Family Church with
some of its projects

Coffee mornings
Global mission
Pastoral care

Prayer Groups
Outreach
Praise
Open Ears
(Informal
Counselling)
Holy Communion

A range of community care
services provided by our
church within the borough

Midweek children's activity group

Alpha house groups

Made by Beryl Gray and Marjorie Kett
assisted by Peter Kett
Regular worshippers stitched their
names on the green leaves
Greenleaf Road Baptist Church

In this Pentecost lectern fall the flames are lurex with iron-on Vilene adhered with bondaweb

In this Easter banner the figures were copied from the Good News Bible and enlarged on a photocopier

My Journey into Banner-Making

I visited a friend in a banner group and was inspired to make a lectern fall for the lectern our family gave to our church in memory of my husband Gordon.

I discovered a banner-making course that takes place every December and have taken advantage of this every year since. The group has enjoyed wonderful experiences creating banners mainly for use in our Churches over Christmas. We share fun, frustration and great Christian fellowship and literally 'burn up the midnight oil' as we do our sewing. It is the highlight of my year.

Usually I work alone and am very fortunate that my church is happy for me to express my own ideas. Most of my work is thematic for the Christian year.

Pamela Powell – Berkswich Methodist Church

Wanaka, Central Otago, New Zealand

Celebrating 150 Years

In a collage and as many stitches as possible, the banner tells the story of our church family and history, our mountains and South Alps, particularly Mt. Aspiring, our lakes, Wanaka and Hawea. It was created by the women of the Upper Clutha Presbyterian Parish in Wanaka, Hawea, Tarras and Luggate in honour of the 150th anniversary of the Synod of Otago and Southland of the Presbyterian Church of Aotearoa (New Zealand).

It hangs in St. Andrew's Presbyterian Church.

Weddington, Nuneaton, Warwickshire

Our group at St. James Church, none of whom are professional embroiderers, was formed with the ideas of making banners to enhance worship within the Church, focus people's thoughts on God and beautify the building. Banners are not, primarily, to communicate pleasing ideas but to present the Word of God. We use the Bible for reference and our designs are born out of prayer. We have found our work a way of expressing our love for God and sharing that love.

Advent Altar Frontal

Advent calls us to prepare ourselves for Christ's coming. The candles represent his coming at Christmas; the chalice, corn and grapes his coming to each one of us at communion in the bread and wine; the middle section looks forward to his coming again, when His presence will fill the world. The waves in the background connect the three panels, indicating movement and the eternal process of Christ's coming to us.

The background fabric was constructed using many different kinds of materials machined together. Other techniques include embroidery, machine embroidery and padded appliqué. The frame is quilted to add interest and to enhance the feeling of God's movement through time.

Christmas Altar Frontal

On the left three wise men come to worship the boy King. In his hands he bears gifts for mankind – His life (the cross) and His Spirit (the dove). The mists of time connect then and now, symbolising that these gifts are for all time. In the left background are the roofs and minarets of the Middle East.

On the right are the figures symbolising modern man and his family with a background of St. James Church and the dwindling industries around.

In the foreground the crocuses point to the new life that comes with Jesus and refer to Isaiah 35:1, 2 – 'The desert and the parched land will be glad; the wilderness will rejoice and blossom. Like the crocus, it will burst into bloom'.

To achieve the colouring in the background, the fabric was painted with car spray paints. Padded appliqué, some machine decoration and hand embroidery were used and net provided the required shading.

Weddington, Nuneaton, Warwickshire

Lent and Holy Week Altar Frontal

The symbols of Christ's suffering surround the cross – the nails, dice, whip and thirty pieces of silver, Judas' betrayal money. The small thorn shapes represent the crown of thorns, the larger ones the sins of mankind pressing in on Christ and causing his death. It helps to bring us to feelings of sorrow and our need for repentance and forgiveness.

The middle section of the frontal was worked in long and short stitch on canvas, padded appliqué and beads were also used.

Easter Altar Frontal

An explosion of light represents the glory of the resurrected Christ breaking in on the world, helping us to experience the joy of Easter morning. Appliqué is used on gold brocade, with satins, cottons, metallic fabrics and beads. The cross is crocheted from string dyed in tea.

Pentecost Frontal

At Pentecost the Church celebrates the coming of the Holy Spirit. Doves and flames are used as symbols of the Holy Spirit. The words and design come from the Book of Acts, chapters 1 & 2. Padded appliqué was used throughout.

Our Design Plan

When designing a banner we always start with the question 'What is the message we are trying to convey?' Preliminary to a group discussion sketches are made, pictures and books gathered and we all pray. Round the table in the home where we meet these are pooled and a vague idea of the finished banner emerges. As we talk more ideas and sketches are forthcoming. Different members bring different skills but all have input.

A full size paper mock up is made. Drawings of the motifs are cut out, placed on the background, positions moved, sizes altered. Material swatches give an idea of colour and texture. A photo-copier is used to enlarge or reduce. Paper patterns and sometimes carbon paper are used to transfer design to material.

Maureen Grant and friends, St. James Church, Weddington

Benedicite Hangings

The Benedicite, one of the traditional Canticles in the Prayer book in praise of creation, inspired this set of hangings,

Backgrounds of numbers 1–5 were constructed by stitching together horizontal bands of fabric – velvets, satins etc. Designs were applied using different techniques, including hand embroidery. The background of number 6 was hand painted on cotton. Number 7 was hand painted and stitched on canvas. The animals and birds (number 7) were hand painted using fabric paint, padded, stitched and cut out before being applied. The background for number 8 was constructed using vertical bands of velvet and gold fabric, designed to take the eye upward in praise. Ribbon embroidery was used for the lettering.

The word 'Ever' extends beyond the edge to indicate that the praise of God cannot be contained within the confines of a banner.

Maureen Grant and friends

Prayer for God's Help in Creativity

Call on me and I will answer (Jeremiah 33:3)

Father *you have given us the mind of Christ. May we listen to him and to what he is saying to us for the church and the world. We come willingly. Enable us together to use the gifts you have given us in your service. We offer you our minds, our hearts and our hands.*

Lord Jesus *thank you for the colours in your world, for primulas and bluebells, poppies and dahlias; for the peacock and the parrots, for the zebra and the lion. Thank you too for the shapes of spider's webs and autumn leaves, the sizes of the bumble-bee and the elephant. Help us to show something of your beauty and joy in the work we do. Amen.*

Lord Jesus *we live in a hurting world. May we receive words and designs from yourself to comfort and strengthen those in loss and pain. May we at other times challenge others to give and to go. Amen.*

Holy Spirit *inspire us so to create that beyond our efforts, the glory of Christ may be seen and His purposes fulfilled. Amen.*

He guides the humble in what is right and teaches them his way (Psalm 25:9)

We have received the Spirit who is from God (1 Corinthians 2:12)

We have the mind of Christ (1 Corinthians 2:16)

These banners were designed by Angela Curror, as a visual expression of a personal longing, and were made by the banner making group. The background sky and sand is polyester cotton fabric, with wool-mix rocks, netting water and felt palm trees. The bones at the bottom of 'O God my soul thirsts for you' and all the lettering on both banners were made from self adhesive felt. Cord was used to define the outline of the sand dunes.

Angela Curror and friends, Christchurch, West Croydon

The dull background of the desert and sky wonderfully evokes the parched and barren landscape. The colour of backgrounds creates the mood, light and darkness, warmth and cold, solemnity and joy, conflict and peace, humility and Majesty. Backgrounds need to contrast with the lettering and to enhance the design and it is good have a variety of colours if several banners are made.

A Gift for Romania

This banner was taken as a gift for Romania by members of the New Life Church, Woking. The verse is 'Those who sow in tears shall reap with songs of joy'. (Psalm 126:5)

The banner being presented to the Romanians (right) by two members of New Life Church, Woking.

The banner is hung for the first time in the church in the village of Marka near Oradea.

Wendy Poupart,
New Life Church

119

Where the Spirit of the Lord is there is freedom

Potent Images   As an artist I find banners a powerful medium for raising expectation in worship. Relating easily to their visual impact I enjoy their theatricality and boldness, my spirit often lifting as I draw near to the Lord in worship. They have a silent ministry, spirit responding to Spirit, by-passing the mind. Like the old advert, they 'reach the parts others cannot reach'. The potency of the visual word should never be underestimated.

Working Together   Having at first denied God's call on my life to lead the Banner Group, I eventually gave in and found myself in the thick of things, working alongside co-leader Shirley.

The first thing I grasped was the importance of our life together. The vision of St. Michael's at that time was for Mission springing from loving, caring, relationships. 'We have nothing more to share with the world, than what we are sharing with each other' (Jim Wallace), was regularly quoted. The group learnt much about the importance of this from Anne Watson, our elder. She also taught us not just to share our joys and sorrows, but to be accountable to one another, listening for God's word for our church and each other. The former, without the latter, can drag you down. Together, they build you up. Sharing lives openly and honestly releases creativity. One can be 'wrong' without fear of rejection and ideas can be freely expressed. This is so refreshing. Honesty about what we think or feel is very precious and empowering. Group members no longer claim individual ownership of banners; seeking God's word and His ideas becomes all-important.

Prophetic Banners   Sometime later, God gave me a glimpse of what he wanted to do through our banners as I listened to a talk on Habakkuk 3. I realised they could be not just aids to worship but worship itself. The response is 'what a great God', not 'what a great prayer'.

The Lord put in me a longing to create banners like that, prophetic banners coming straight from God's heart, pointing to him and proclaiming 'what a great God', not 'what a great banner'. God had spoken to the group many times in the past with words of comfort and encouragement for the church, but I sensed this was a new season. We were being asked to enter into the realm of 'prophetic' banners, expressing His innermost longing, sharing His tears and echoing His laughter. Now left in sole leadership of the group, it was up to me to pass on this vision, but how? The opportunity to find out soon came with our next set of banners for Pentecost – 'Where the Spirit of the Lord is there is Freedom'.

Stimulating the Imagination   When exploring new ideas I like to stimulate as many of our senses as possible, so I put a bunch of spring flowers, a candle and a white dove on the table on which to meditate. We lit the candle, but were soon aware that the first Pentecost had been far more dynamic than our wavering flame – we needed a proper fire.

Next week we met around Ruth's kitchen range to watch the real thing. We soon found that damp logs don't burn. Adding fire-lighters and sticks and with much blowing and flapping, we coaxed a flickering flame. Next came the smoke, lots of it! It was no coincidence that our first ideas featured spirals of blue-grey smoke! Eventually we sat in the dark watching a roaring fire. The Lord showed us many things about life in the Spirit that night, not least, that even the smallest spark shines in the darkness.

The Pentecost Banners, St. Michael-le-Belfrey, York. The congregation was preparing to take part in 'Songs of Praise'.

121

York

Prayer and Fasting   For our next three or four meetings, in the tradition of the ancient icon painters, we prayed and fasted. Then we studied God's word, poring over the works of the Holy Spirit in the Old and New Testaments. Images of flames and doves for Pentecost seemed all too obvious, the need to dig deeper spurred us on.

Learning to be attentive to 'those little butterflies that flit across your mind's eye' (John Wimber), whilst pottering around my kitchen, an image flew in and out again. A spiral of flames turning into a flock of doves. I stored it away for the right time.

Recurring Images   Next week as we met to share ideas, guess what? The same image came up again and again! The Lord had spoken to us all individually. A further idea of a dove caught in a thicket, or cage, set us thinking that there might be more to come. As the group prayed for clarification, I asked the Lord for a word for our church. It came. John 7:9 speaks of the disciples lack of power and gives this reason – 'for as yet the Spirit had not been given (to the believers) because Jesus was not yet glorified'. The 'glory' which John referred to was the death and resurrection of Jesus. Until Jesus is glorified in our church we, too, would be powerless.

So how did this relate to our ideas? I suddenly realised that the bird was not flying from a thicket, but a crown of thorns. The release of power at Pentecost was only made possible by the death and obedience of Jesus at Calvary. From the symbol of death, the crown of thorns, sprang the symbols of power and love, the flames and the doves.

Sovereign Confirmation   That weekend God gave us two further 'pictures' sovereignly confirming our ideas. I came across a C.N.D. leaflet advertising an Easter march, depicting three doves flying up and off to the right from a crown of thorns. Then Ruth, oblivious of our ideas, returned from holiday with a C.N.D. postcard called 'Peace'. Fired from a gun bottom left, spiralling blue smoke released a dove top right! We soon got the message and set to work.

The first of the two large banners depicts a crown of thorns with flames leaping and spiralling upwards, ending in a flurry of white doves. The second bears the scripture 'Where the Spirit of the Lord is there is freedom'. In addition, we made six small banners with crowns of thorns and ever-increasing flames.

That autumn the new banners went to Sweden on a mission with our choir. It turned out to be an amazing time. God released His Spirit and it was a turning point for many. Back in York His Spirit was poured out too, simultaneously with two teams visiting other parts of this country. There was much rejoicing when we all gathered back in York, not least from the banner group as we saw our 'prophecy' fulfilled.

Gill Douglas and friends, St. Michael-le-Belfrey

Christ Has Set Us Free

God often works out banner themes in our lives. The 'picture' on which this banner was based was given out to our church during a service. It took the group only three weeks to make. Each week we came in and speculated as to which balloon we were and whether we were stuck in the clouds or flying high! At the same time we were working on a set of seven banners on holiness. They took us eighteen months to complete!

Gill Douglas and friends, St. Michael-le-Belfrey

God's Fragrance Set Free

We can only give to the world as much as we have amongst ourselves. It was when the alabaster box of ointment was broken open that the perfume flowed (Mark 14:3). As we share our lives in love and commitment we too are broken and God's fragrance is set free in our churches and in the world. The quality of our banner is a direct reflection of where we are with God and with each other. We can have lovely designs and beautiful craftsmanship, but the resulting banners can be empty unless we have the right foundations. Our willingness to allow God to work in our relationships allows His Spirit to flow. As we draw close to Him and to each other so He is able to speak to us and anoint our gifts.

Gill Douglas

Banners – where now?

Is banner making entering a new era? The enthusiasm of the many contributors to this book is a sign that its popularity is not diminished. It is difficult to get a clear picture of what is happening but there are many current issues and trends that may impinge on this ministry.

• *Here in the UK women (the mainstay of banner groups) are juggling home-making with employment and have less time to offer. However, there are ways to create more quickly or alternatively a year-long project is a possibility.*

• *A generation of women who were brought up to sew, make clothes, knit and crochet, have not always passed on their skills. At the same time art and design in textiles has become an increasing area of interest.*

• *The presence of the latest technology in many churches means that images, both still and moving, can be part our experience and enhance the teaching and worship. Used well it can be powerful and provoking.*

• *Installations are popular today in the art world. Some churches have broadened out from the customary vase of flowers to erecting structures that can be very challenging: eliciting powerful responses, speaking to our unconscious in a way that words cannot reach, and asking the existential questions. An example would be not just talking about the potter and the clay, but actually bringing in a potter's wheel, having an array of pots, both whole and broken at the front of the church.*

• *In the contemporary art world, we notice that paintings have become less realistic, leaving more to the imagination. This trend may be reflected in future banner designs. Who can tell in what ways the Holy Spirit will inspire further creativity?*

• *In the banner world the challenge is to make banners for the present and to let go of those that are tired and worn. At the same time the importance of recycling may help us to use scraps and old resources in imaginative new ways.*

• *Banner-making has usually been a separate ministry. It is possible now to envisage involvement with a wider group of people enjoying creativity together in more diverse ways. Perhaps this could take place at a special festival or celebration in which drama, dance, flower arrangements, installations, banner, music and computer technology (or some of these!) combine to enrich worship?*

Rosas Mitchell

Resources

The cost of materials

Many groups find their churches willing to support financially. The cost of banners is usually much less than other aspects of church life. Sometimes people contribute from their own store (see Prestwick's story).

Rainbow Silks – Highly recommended. Silk painting and textile decoration, calligraphy, screen printing, collage and more, with a wide range of books. Speedy and knowledgeable mail order. Well-stocked shop with supplies for a wide range of crafts including textile arts, collage, jewellery and more. Creative classes held in their own studios.
Mail order: 6 Wheelers Yard, Great Missenden, Buckinghamshire, HP16 0AL
Shop: 85 High Street, Great Missenden, Buckinghamshire, HP16 0AL
Telephone: 01494 862111 See website www.rainbowsilks.co.uk or ask for catalogue (64 pages costs £2.00)
Email: caroline@rainbowsilks.co.uk

Mandors Fabric Store, Fleming House, 134 Renfrew Street, Glasgow G3 6ST
Huge Fabric and haberdashery departments including patchwork and curtain materials. Mail order service – phone in and pay by credit card. Samples available by sending a cheque for £2.50 (£5.00 for bridal and evening wear fabrics) and 5 will be sent.
Telephone: 0141 332 7716 Website: www.mandors.co.uk Email: fabric@mandors.co.uk

Borovick Fabrics Ltd. is an Aladdin's cave of hundreds of fabrics supplied for fashion, stage, screen and TV and church needlework. They only supply fabrics and threads. There is no catalogue, but write with specific details of the type of fabric, colour and use sending a SAE. They will send samples with prices and widths.
16 Berwick Street, London W1F 0HP
Telephone: 020 7437 2180/0520; Fax: 020 7494 4646 Email: borovickfabrics@btclick.com

Fabricland – shops in 10 different towns and cities in south of England. Wide range of fabrics but not much in curtain material. Mail order service. Head office in Ringwood.
Telephone: 01425 461444
Website: www.fabricland.co.uk

Hobbycraft Shops – 28 shops, all in England except one in Newport, Wales. There is no catalogue but shops will post goods. Telephone: 0800 027 2387 Website: www.hobbycraft.co.uk

Whaleys (Bradford) Ltd. Natural fibre fabrics, flameproofed fabrics, stage/theatrical drapes. Free brochure.
Telephone 01274 576718 Website: www.whaleys-bradford.ltd.uk Email: whaleys@btinternet.com

J. D. McDougall – Stage & screen suppliers of large pieces of canvas or material
4 McGrath Road, London E15 4JP
Telephone: 020 8534 2921 Website: www.mcdougall.co.uk – online catalogue. Email: mail@mcdougall.co.uk

Turley Textiles, Regalia Mills, Hollings Street, Cottingley, West Yorkshire BD16 1SH
Suppliers of clerical, academic and theatrical textiles. Will send samples.
Telephone: 01274 551700 Website: www.turleytextiles.co. uk

Silk fabrics, packs of colour co-ordinated silk pieces or silk by the metre may be obtained from
The Silk Route, Cross Cottage, Cross Lane, Frimley Green, Surrey GU16 6LN
Telephone: 01252 835781 Email: hilary@thesilkroute.co.uk

Oliver Twists – hand-dyed threads, fabrics and fibres. Detailed leaflet available.
22 Phoenix Road, Washington, Tyne & Wear NE38 0AD
Telephone: 0191 416 6016 Fax: 0191 415 3405 Email: jean@olivertwists.freeserve.co.uk

Barnyarns, Canal Wharf, Bondgate Green, Ripon HG4 1AQ
Retail shop and mail order – gold kid, embroidery and metallic threads, etc.

Telephone: 01765 690069 Email: sales@barnyarns.co.uk

Colour prints for cards (some groups have made cards and bookmarks with photos of their banners). Four photos can be copied on to an A4 sheet, cut and stuck on to home-made cards.

Thought Factory – Postcards can be made from banner photos – minimum 250. Telephone: 0116 276 5302
Website: www.thoughtfactory.co.uk   Email: sales@thoughtfactory.co.uk

Guild of Silk Painters – helpful both for beginners and those more experienced. Many branches and an attractive journal produced four times a year. Email: membership@silkpaintersguild.co.uk www.silkpainters-guild.co.uk

International Craft and Hobby Fair Ltd. They organise Creative Stitches & Hobbycrafts Exhibitions in different venues throughout the year. Phone for a leaflet.
Telephone: 01425 272711 Website: www.ichf.co.uk   Email: info@ichf.co.uk

Books on Banners

Banners for All Seasons – how to make creative banners for holy days and holidays – by Joyce Pike and Anne Robinson. Meriwether Publishing Ltd. This book describes in detail the making of 15 banners for various occasions. It is beautifully illustrated with pages in colour ISBN 9781566080590 £10.99

Banners with Pizazz – a step-by-step guide by Diane Guelzow. Resource Publications Inc.
A practical book full of ideas, pictures, attractive lettering and design – mostly black and white.
ISBN 089390208X £11.50

The New Banner Book by Betty Wolfe. Morehouse Publishing. Another practical book with many ideas for symbols, design and lettering. Mostly black and white. ISBN 0819217816 £9.99

A Poster Book
Prepare the Way with Posters by Yvonne Coppock. Gazelle Books. This book is about making posters to place outside the church to attract passers by. It gives many helpful ideas with paper and other mediums. It is only available from Yvonne at 7 Belvedere Drive, St. Saviour, Jersey JE2 7RN
Telephone: 01534 737171
Website: www.postersplus.org.uk
Email: ycoppock@localdial.com
ISBN 1 899746188 £10.99 includes p&p.

Your local Christian bookshop will be able to find out about other Banner Books in print.

The Batsford series of craft and embroidery books are recommended.

Books on Silk Painting
An Introduction to Silk Painting by Jill Kennedy (privately published but available from Rainbow Silks)
Beginners Guide to Silk Painting by Mandy Southan. Publisher: Search Press ISBN 0855328029

Many excellent books can be obtained from the library.

The following magazine carries a wide selection of mail order suppliers.
Workbox magazine – features on a variety of textile themes and techniques including embroidery, quilting, beadwork and news and information from around the UK. Available from newsagents. One copy available from Ebony Media Ltd, PO Box 25, Liskeard, Cornwall PL14 6XX. Telephone: 01579 340100
£2.75 includes p&p.

Sharing skills
Many banner-makers have shared skills with others by informal meetings, talks and workshops. Some people from different places get together for banner days.

Open to Commissions

The following people work on a professional basis and are available for commissions:

Yvonne Bell is a Christian painter and vestment designer. Her work can be seen on the website of the Guild of Silk Painters – www.silkpainters-guild.co.uk
Telephone/Fax: 01908 623474 Website: www.vestments.co.uk Email: yvonnebell@yvonnebell.co.uk

Melitta Bosworth is willing to facilitate the making of banners – either by running workshops to support groups and their ideas or by working to commission. She is also willing to facilitate Art and Prayer workshops exploring our faith experiences and ideas. Telephone: 01738 623273 Email: melittaart@aol.com
The Bield Retreat Centre at Blackruthven, Tibbermore, Perth PH1 1PY (Scotland)
E mail: info@bieldatblackruthven.org.uk

Juliet Hemingray leads a team of 13 making banners and vestments to order for the UK and overseas.
The Derwent Business Centre, Clarke Street, Derby DE1 2BU
Telephone: 01332 366740 Website: www.church-textiles.co.uk Email: jh@church-textiles.co.uk

Carol Marples (not represented in this book) is involved in a wider ministry than just banners – 'Soul Marks'. She seeks to encourage and enable churches, organisations, groups and individuals, by the provision of professional guidance and training, to be creative and challenging in using the senses, particularly the visual arts to express, communicate, stimulate and inspire faith in God.
Telephone: 0131 467 6243 Website: www.soulmarks.co.uk Email: carol@carolmarples.co.uk

Surfing the internet for Praise and Worship Banners

There are different ways to search the internet for finished banners or supplies. In the USA many banners are bought ready-made from manufacturers.

There are different search engines but Google and A9 are noteworthy in that they will search the web for pictures also. Searches can be restricted by country and sometimes locality. Suitable words used when searching yield multiple results. For instance, using the words 'praise banners', a list of 12 websites were identified. If you try the same words later you may find a completely different list of websites. This is because of the ever-changing way the search engines rank the sites or because of marketing efforts by the website owners. Some search engines rank sites by the number of people who view them. Even it you don't want to buy the banners (some are available only in the USA), there is a vast resource for inspiration for your own designs. Happy surfing.

Alan Lowne – New York State, USA.

Snowflake banner

The snowflakes were made from firm white fabric. To make one – take a square of fabric, fold it four times and then cut the patterns with scissors. Glue to strong background.

'The blood of Jesus, His Son, purifies us from all sin.' (1 John 1:7)

'For God so loved the world that He gave His one and only Son that whoever believes in Him shall not perish but have everlasting life.' (John 3:16)

Were the whole realm of nature mine,
That were an offering far too small –
Love so amazing, so divine
Demands my soul, my life, my all.

(Isaac Watts)